MW01697917

Dedication

I dedicate this book to my wife, my son, my sisters, my aunts and uncles, my cousins, my nieces and nephews, my friends and neighbors.

I would like to thank my teachers from first grade to graduate school who taught me how to think, observe, think critically, assess, and learn.

Special Thanks

I am grateful for all the technology that made our current life possible. I used these technologies to write this book. I would like to extend a special thanks to Microsoft Office, Google.com, Yahoo.com, Wikipedia.com, Dictionary.com, Rymezone.com, Canstockphotos.com, Storybook.com, and others. Of course, I must thank the Internet and the hardware that these software and services run on. Without these tools; this book would not have been possible.

Book was edited by Haadi Marashi - Thanks

Pondering & Wondering

Sharing Thoughts and Ideas by Musa Marashi

2nd Edition

October 2020

$21.99
ISBN 978-1-7347849-0-9
52199>
9 781734 784909

Printed by:
Pushpanshu Kumar |Asian Paper Products |
ISO 9001:2015 Certified Company|
Email: asianpaperproducts@gmail.com |
Website: https://www.indiamart.com/asianpaperproducts/about-us.html |
Corporate Office:
C-46, First Floor, DDA Shed, Okhla Phase-1, New Delhi-110020 | INDIA
Phone: +91- 8802332530 | **Whats App No. :** +91- 8802332530 |

Musa Marashi
Email: musa.marashi@gmail.co
Website: musa-marashi.com

Table of Contents

Preface

Since my childhood, I was enamored of reading and writing. I read many classical Arabic and Persian books as well as many translated novels written by various renowned international authors. I read, Le Misérables, War and Peace, and several of Ernest Hemingway's novels by the age of 17. I liked movies, especially comedy. I enjoyed Indian films (Bollywood productions).

I love Persian and Arabic poetry. As a matter of fact, in our family circle, poetry was used as a form of entertainment. People in the Middle East respected poets. As a sign of sophistication, people strive to memorize poems and recite them at the appropriate occasions.

During the summer months, it does not rain in Baghdad Iraq. Days are very hot, but the nights are cool in the open spaces. The night sky is unadulterated by the city lights. It has an awesome three-dimensional view of a sky full of sparkling stars. Taking advantage of this phenomena, people used to spread their mattresses on the floor of the flat roof of their houses after sunset to cool off before they were ready to go to bed.

In our family we used to have a summer ritual. We would gather in a circle and play games or to tell stories. One of our favorite games, when we had guests, was to challenge each other with poetry. So, we used to huddle in a circle at the edge of the mattresses and play the game. The lead person starts with one line of a poem and asks the next person in the circle to recite a line from another poem that starts with the letter that the previous line of poem ended with. (Arabic is a phonetic language). The process continues until people get eliminated one by one or get exhausted and are ready to go to sleep.

This environment instilled a love of poetry and literature in me. I used to pretend to be an author and publish my own books. I was eight years old and published 9 books. These books were simple handwritten scribbles on pieces of papers that were sewn in the middle to look like a book. Later, when I was 12 years old, I.

Preface

began publishing a magazine. It had a circulation of 6 –my mother, brother, my sister, my uncle, and a couple of cousins.
I always dreamed of having a typewriter so that I could present my magazine like a real magazine –(This was in late 1950s and early 1960s). When I came to the US, this dream came to fruition. I bought a typewriter, which I needed for my term papers, but unfortunately, I did not have enough mastery of the language (English) to write poetry or stories.

I wrote several short stories when I was in my early twenties when I was in Iran. I tried to publish them, but they were rejected by a couple of magazines that I sent the stories to.

As I went through school and read news papers and magazines, I became very fond of the English language. It is rich, expressive, and beautiful. From time to time, I made an attempt to rekindle the desire to express my views and feeling in my new adopted language, but work and other commitments dampened this fire. Now that I am approaching retirement, I felt compelled to share my thoughts and feelings with my fellow Americans and World citizens.

My poetry style is perhaps not what the reader is accustomed to. It is heavily influence by the Eastern Style of writing poetry. Rhyme and symmetry is very important in the Arabic and Persian poems. My poems are a mix of styles. I hope you find them acceptable.

My more urgent hope is that you would read my articles that deal with conflicts in the world. I truly believe that in this day and age and at the dawn of a new millennium, we can solve our problems in a rational and civilized way.

Musa Marashi

October 2020

Bio

I was born in Kadimeyyah, a suburb of Baghdad, Iraq in 1945. My father used to trade between Iraq and Iran and hence, we moved back and forth between Iran and Iraq. I lived a total of 11 years in Iran and 12 years in Iraq. I came to the United States on October 8th, 1970 to pursue my education.

During that period, the country was involved in the Vietnam War., the economy was doing well, and Mr. Nixon was the president. Much has gone on in the last fifty years. The people have changed, the country has changed, and many things have happened in this interval -wars, inventions, and others major events.

I watch and observed what goes on in the country and the world. It is fascinating to see and hear about the events of the day. Politic, discoveries, drama, social events, trends, sports, music, movies, etc.

I lived through 24 US federal elections, nine presidencies, three presidential impeachment efforts, one presidential resignation, one vice presidential resignation, and several turn overs of congressional and supreme court powers through elections or by assignments. I lived in New Jersey for this entire period and saw change overs of governorship from democrat to republican and vice versa.

Bio *continued*

I also lived through the Vietnam war, two Iraqi wars, the Afghanistan war, and couple of smaller wars –the Granada, and Panama wars. The Arab-Israeli war of 1973, the Iran-Iraq war, the Indian-Pakistani war, the Northern Ireland conflict, the Georgia-Russian war, the Falkland Islands war, etc. There were many horrible terrorist events that killed hundreds. The worst was the attack of September 11 on the World Trade Centers in New York in 2001.

There were several scandals –Watergate, Iran-Gate, the Lewinsky affair, Russia's interference in the 2016 election, and others that did not involve the presidents. There were many corruption cases on the federal and local levels.

I lived through many historical events –The downing of the Berlin Wall, the release of Nelson Mandala, the dissolution of the Apartheid system in South Africa, the Polish uprising, the breakup of the Soviet Union, The Revolution in Iran, the Arab Spring, and more.

There were many t ragic and sad events. Deaths of stars, a princess, celebrities, and many happy events as well. Several Olympics, World Cups, royal weddings, and the historical event of the election of the first

Bio *continued*

African-American president and first woman contender for the presidency.

Among the most painful events of recent years is the gun violence that permeating our society. The shooting of the innocent children of Sandy Hook Elementary School in December 2012. The economic collapse of 2008 was another shocker. The political posturing and stagnation of partisan politic is nauseating.

I saw much good in this period as well. I witnessed the introductions of personal computers, cell phones and smart-phones, GPS devices, Microsoft software and tools, Google, Yahoo, Facebook, twitter, and LinkedIn. Of course these are the technologies I am familiar with. There are many other advances in the medical area, transportation, construction, food processing, retail industries, banking and finance, and other countless innovations and inventions.

I came to the United States in 1970 in pursuit of education. I also was a man without a country. A year earlier, I was forced to leave my country of birth Iraq to go to Iran, where five years earlier, my family escaped from Iran fearing the security police of the Shah. I came to the US without any of my records, so I had to start from scratch. I went to night school to

Bio *continued*

prepare for my high school equivalency diploma and to improve my English. I got my diploma from Hackensack High School in Bergen County, New Jersey. Then I attended Bergen Community College part-time. A year later, I enrolled in a full program to get my Associates Degree in Science. I graduated in May of 1975. Then I transferred to Fairleigh Dickinson University in Teaneck, New Jersey and got my Bachelor of Science in Computer Science in December of 1977 and Master of Science in Computer Science in 1978.

I started work as a computer science professional in June of 1977 for Systems and Programming International (SPI), Tenafly, New Jersey, a consulting company which had a contract with IT&T in New York.

In October 1980, I worked for AT&T Bell Laboratories in Holmdel, New Jersey. I started my own company called Code Technology, Inc. (CTI) and was subcontracting through SPI at Bell Labs. While working at Bell Labs, I was also working on side projects through CTI.

CTI was a Computer Consulting and Software Development company.

Bio *continued*

After three and half years, I moved on and started working as direct consultant for AT&T and Bell Labs. I also worked for Telcordia Technologies on the Y2K project for 2 years. I stopped consulting in mid-2003. However, I had a staff of 20 or so people working in our company.

Since 1994, our Company focused its effort on Internet applications and had acquired over 140 domains to provide services for individuals and businesses.

Working as a consultant and running my own little company, did not leave much time for socializing. My consulting work often involved travel both nationwide and abroad.

I got married late in life. I was 50 years when I got married in November of 1996. I met my wife Nidhal in London, while working on behalf of one of my clients, through my cousin who lives there. She had just graduated from Kings College with PhD in Chemistry. She moved to the United States in March of 1997. She began Teaching Chemistry in various colleges and universities in Central New Jersey.

Bio *continued*

In May 23, 2000, we were blessed with a son, our only child, –Haadi. He is now twenty years old (2020) and attends the New Jersey Institute of Technology, (NJIT) University, in Newark, NJ studying Biomedical Engineering.

I began teaching as an adjunct instructor in several colleges and universities since 2008. I taught Computer Science courses, Math, and the Arabic language.

I am still dreaming of hitting it big. I have several projects that I am working on. I am hoping that these will help society to live a better life. At the moment, I am concentrating on sharing my views with you.

I worked on my first book, "Sharing Thoughts: by Musa Marashi", in mid summer of 2013 and was published the next year. I felt there is a need for me to speak up. I believe I have something important to say. I wanted to share my thoughts with the world. This is the second edition of the book, with some chapters removed.

Musa Marashi

Part A

Living

Life Cycle

March 1993

Life Cycle

March 1993

I am a thought in search of a poem.

I am a poem in search of a song.

I am a song in search of a melody.

I am a melody in search of a guitar.

I am a guitar in search of a touch.

I am a touch in search of a soul.

I am a soul in search of a life.

I am a life in search of a destiny.

I am a destiny in search of the truth.

I am a truth in search of hope.

I am a hope in search of an expression.

I am an expression in search of a feeling.

I am a feeling in search of a thought.

I want to live to be

May 7, 2013

Growing Up

I want to live to be one,

so that I can decide how to have fun.

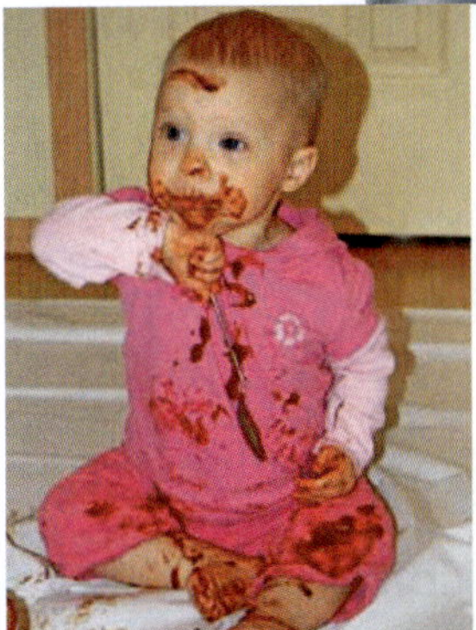

I want to live to be two,

so that I do what I want to do.

I want to live to be three,

so that I pick dandelions and climb tree.

I want to live to be four,

so that I listen to adults no more.

I want to live to be five,

so that I can swim and dive.

I want to live to be six,

so that I can be with the kids and mix.

I want to live to be seven,

so to fly high close to heaven.

I want to live to be eight,

so that I tell no one what I ate.

I want to live to be nine,

so that staying late to be fine.

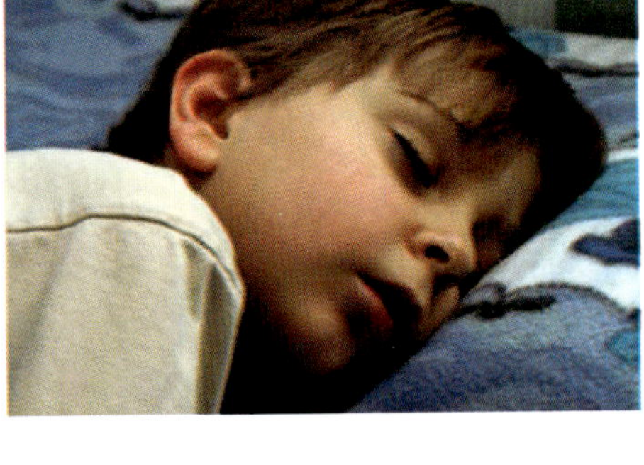

I want to live to be ten,

so to watch plenty TV in the den.

I want to live to be eleven,

so to play games with Donna and Kevin.

I want to live to be twelve,

so in important matters I can delve.

I want to live to be thirteen,

so to be who I am, not to be mean.

I want to live to be fourteen,

so to grow up happy and turn up clean.

I want to live to be fifteen,

so to eat junk, forget about broccoli and bean.

I want to live to be sixteen,

so to date the prettiest chicks you ever seen.

so to date the handsomest guys you ever seen.

I want to live to be seventeen,

so to drive cars, prepare to meet Admission Dean.

I want to live to be eighteen,

so to be away in college with fun in between.

I want to live to be nineteen,

so to face the challenges, drink plenty caffeine.

I want to live to be twenty,

so to be ready to graduate, worries are plenty.

I want to live to be twenty one,

so to say farewell fun; with schooling I'll be done.

I want to live to be twenty five,

so to get a job, a pad, a girl, I shall arrive.

so to get a job, a pad, a guy, I shall arrive.

I want to live to be thirty,

so to marry, climb the ladder, play golf,
hit a birdie.
so to marry, climb the ladder, play tennis
like Christi.

I want to live to be forty,

so to have a home, family, children, and be hefty.

I want to live to be fifty,

so I shall think of retiring, stashing money,
be softie.

I want to live to be sixty,

so the children will be grown, and house will be empty.

I want to live to be seventy,

so I will play with grandchildren,
clean and dirty.

I want to live to be eighty,

so I will be feeling frail, tired, slow, and rusty.

I want to live to be ninety,

so my sight will be weak, my health will be shifty.

I want to live to be a hundred,

so I go back being a child, need to be pampered.

5 Simple Rules for a Happy Life

1. Don't be ~~overly emotional.~~

   =Have faith.

2. Don't ~~ever give up.~~

   =Keep Trying.

3. Don't make things ~~complicated.~~

   =Keep it Simple.

4. Don't take things ~~too seriously~~.

   =Laugh at Problems.

5. Don't be a ~~grown-up.~~

   =Stay as youthful as a kid.

http://rishikajain.com/2012/04/06/5-simple-rules-for-a-happy-life/

Dreaming of Tomorrow

May 12, 2010

Dreaming of Tomorrow

The world around us full of terror,
murder, and gun.
Children dying, people maimed,
scared on the run.
Man loosing wife, girl loosing father,
and mother loosing son.
No end in sight. Will it go away
or has it just begun?

Dreaming of Tomorrow

People anguish, jobs lost, dreams crushed
by the ton.
Lives ruined; hope dwindled, confusion,
so much stun.
Pollutions, angry nature, fires, quakes, and
the rain is not done.
Government paralysis, wasted money,
blame taken by none.

Dreaming of Tomorrow

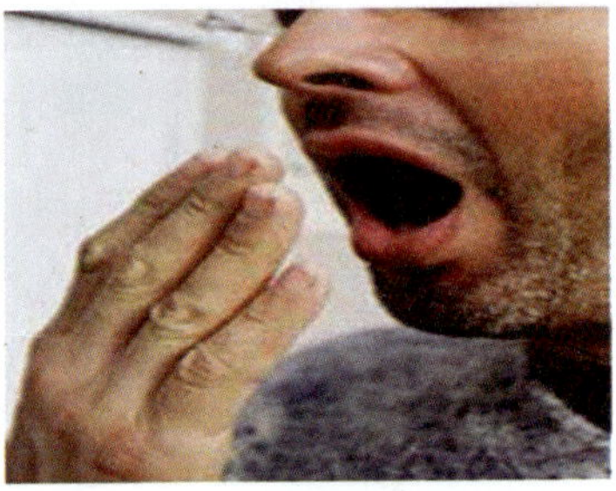

Gloomy clouds of despair no vivacity,
an awful yawn.
We can't see the stars sparkle
or the meteors run.
Obscured daylight, beyond the thick haze
shines the sun.
Overcast nights, behind the clouds the moon
is having fun.

Dreaming of Tomorrow

I am dreaming of a
wonderful tomorrow.
A world void of pain, hurt,
and sorrow.
No despot kings, no cruel leaders,
and no pharaoh.
Enough food, shelter, and clothes,
no need to borrow.

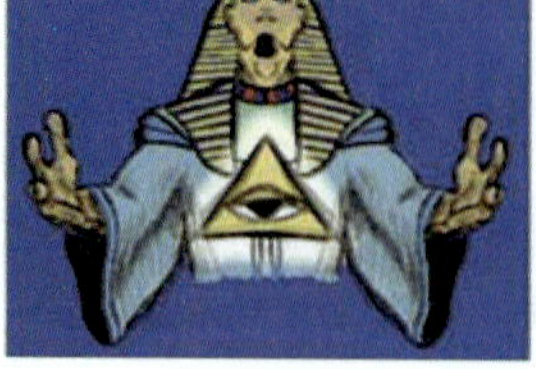

Dreaming of Tomorrow

What I shall speak off has been
already said.
I want every child to be
adequately fed.
No hunger, no pain before
he goes to bed.
Sleeps in peace with the story
has been read.

Dreaming of Tomorrow

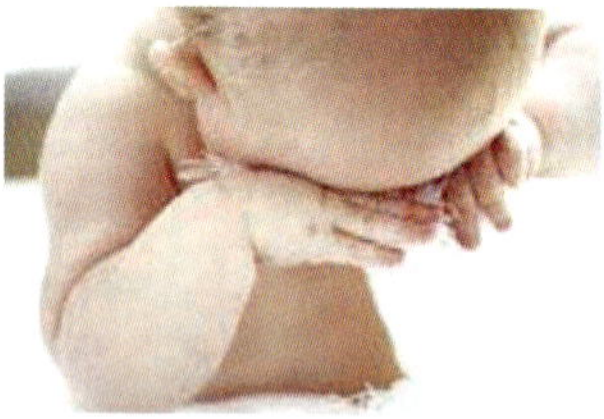

No worries, no hunger, no aches,
and no tears shed.
No broken bones, no injuries,
and no wound bled.
No sleeping on the floor, no missing pillow,
just a decent bed.
No nightmares, no fear of tomorrow,
and no confused head.

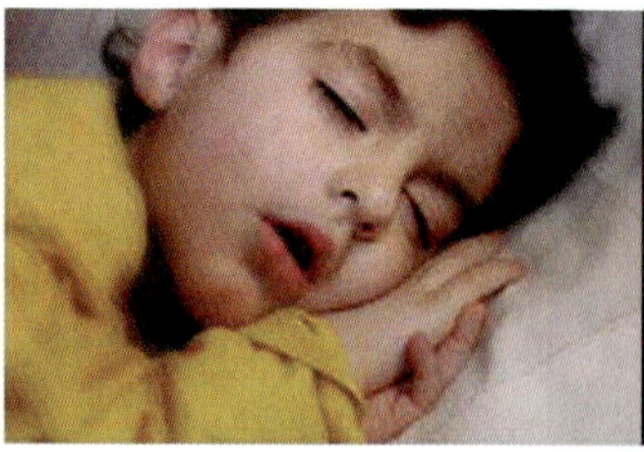

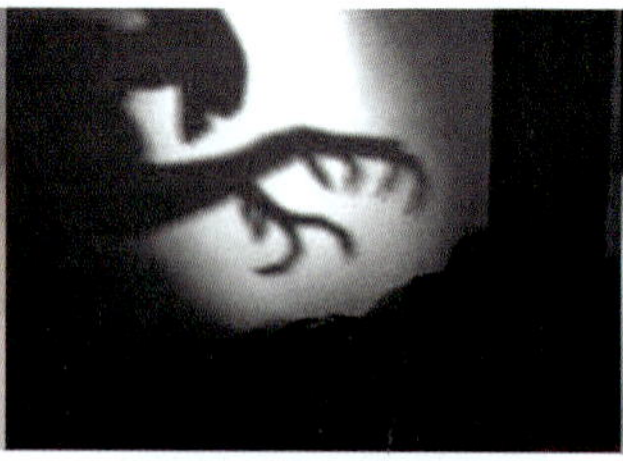

Dreaming of Tomorrow

My dreams, my hopes, my aspirations
is shared by all.
We need to work together in harmony
to move this ball.
No time to waste, let us act now,
let us answer the call.
Yes, the task is great, but we cannot
waver or forestall.

Dreaming of Tomorrow

Let us not just witness what is going on
and be complaining.
We need to act. Enough discussions,
no more explaining.
The sewer of political filth is overflowing
-time for draining.
This is a call for sincere action,
not political campaigning.

YESTERDAY
NOW
TOMORROW

I am a Child

December 18, 2012

Sandy Hook Elementary School shooting

http://en.wikipedia.org/wiki/Sandy_Hook_Elementary_School_shooting

From Wikipedia, the free encyclopedia

On December 14, 2012, 20-year-old Adam Lanza fatally shot twenty children and six adult staff members in a mass murder at Sandy Hook Elementary School in the village of Sandy Hook in Newtown, Connecticut. Before driving to the school, Lanza had shot and killed his mother Nancy at their Newtown home. As first responders arrived, he committed suicide by shooting himself in the head.

All photos were copied from www.google.com/images

I am a Child

This is a message to the politicians coming from the heart.

I am a Child

I am a child; I want to have a long life; this is the start.

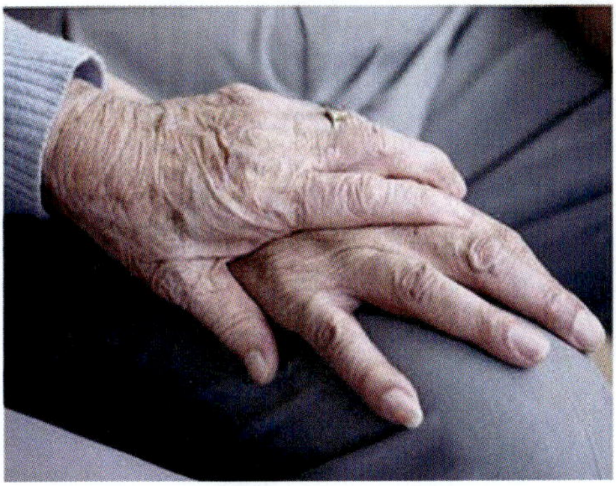

I am a Child

I want to grow happy, have fun, attend school and be smart.

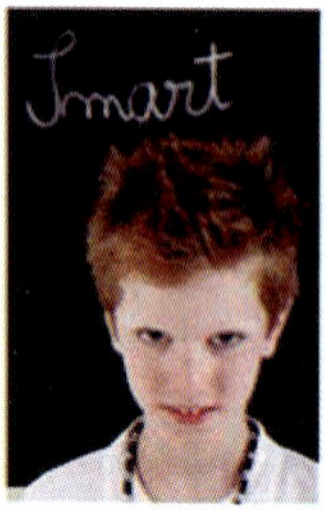

I am a Child

My family and my friends love me, so do I on my part.

I am a Child

Let me live my life. I don't want to be statistics on the chart.

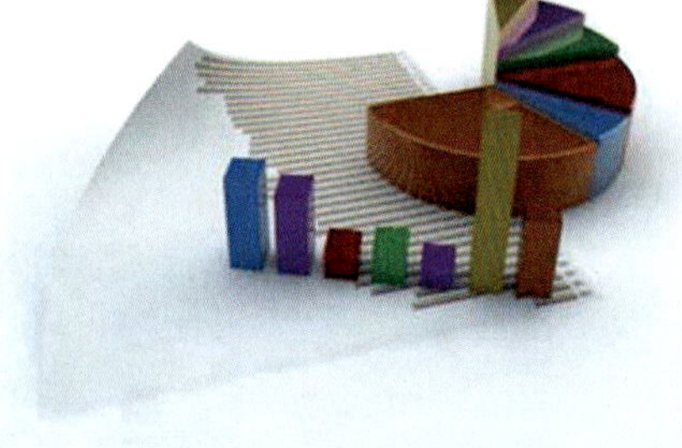

I am a Child

I am the joy of my family. Don't let me be the target of a dart.

I am a Child

Guns kill people. They are tools for murder not a piece of art.

I am a Child

People say, I use them for hunting, but, I am a human not a hart.

I am a Child

At home, school, and the playground, smiles and joy I impart.

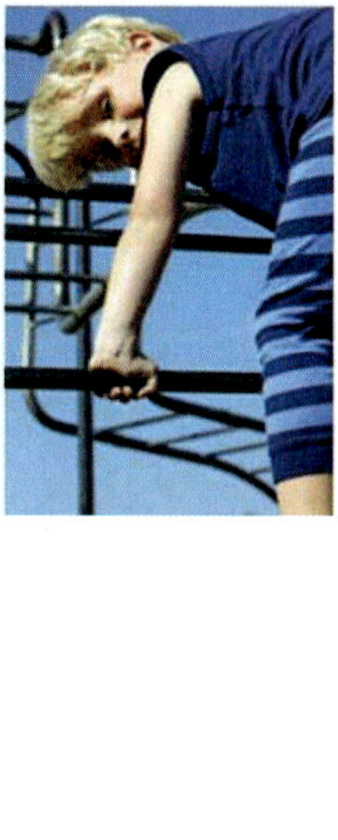

I am a Child

My life ended with gun shots.
Lying dead with Mary and Bart.

Rebels with Cause

All pictures were copied from www.google.com/images

The World Spring

The various peoples protests that led to the overthrow of the Tunisian, Egyptian, Libyan, and Yemini regimes in 2010 through 2012 was dubbed as the Arab Spring.

The people of these countries rebelled against the long ruling dictators that governed them and abused their powers and pillaged the resources of the nation; driving their people to the economic and social abyss. They gathered in the public squares to protest their condition and demanded the removal of the governing regimes.

The response varied from country to country. Old leaders were toppled (exiled, imprisoned, or killed). In many cases, chaos and disorder ensued. The euphoria of victory soon turned into chaos and the various groups, which once were allied, began fighting among themselves seeking control and power. To many, it seemed an old tune being played by different musicians. People's lives did not get better. Their conditions did not improve. To the contrary, they got worse. Outside money and influence contributed to the turmoil and disarray. These nations substituted a singular dictator with a bunch of unruly partisan demagogues. The hope that was sprung from the change turned into the autumn of despair. When would this condition be rectified? No one knows.

A common cry of the protesters in all of these situations was similar. No different than those you hear in some of the countries where they are already blessed with democracy and those who are aspiring to have one. All people of the world want to have the same things. They want freedom, a decent living condition, opportunities to improve their future and the future of their children, and to participate in running their country. I call that –**The World Spring.**

I am a Rebel

August 11, 2013

I am a rebel.

I don't need a gun to kill my brother.

I need loafs of freshly baked bread.

I am a Rebel

I am a rebel.

I need healthcare.

I need medical coverage
from my toes up to my head.

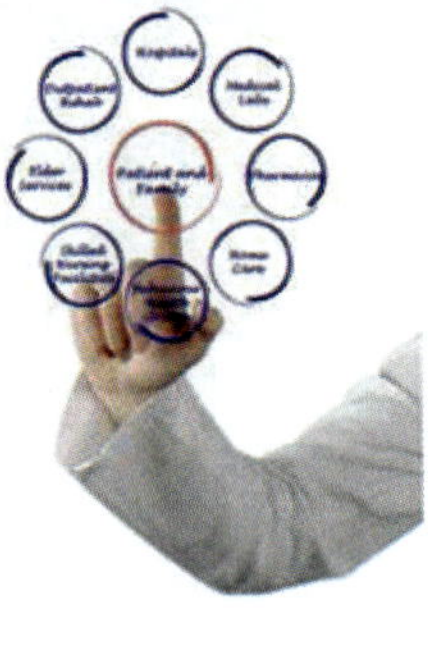

I am a Rebel

I am a rebel.

I need a career.

I need to achieve my goals,
before I am old and dead.

I am a Rebel

I am a rebel.

I need a family.

I need a life partner to love
and to whom I will be wed.

I am a Rebel

I am a rebel.

I need a shelter.

I need a safe house with kitchen, den, and a good bed.

I am a Rebel

I am a rebel.

I need decent cloths to wear.

I need needles and
some colored thread.

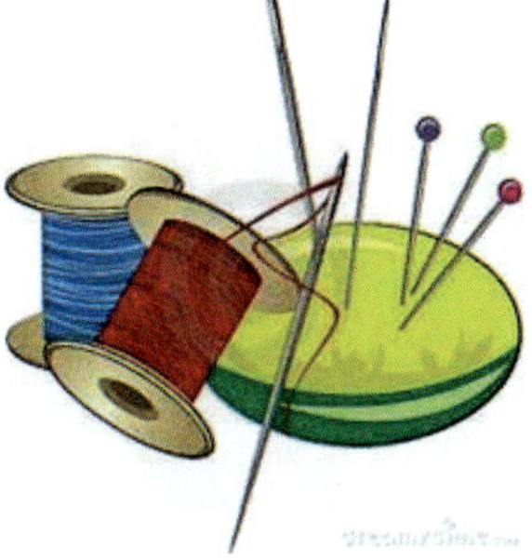

I am a Rebel

I am a rebel.

I need to speak freely.

I need to be free and
hear what is being said.

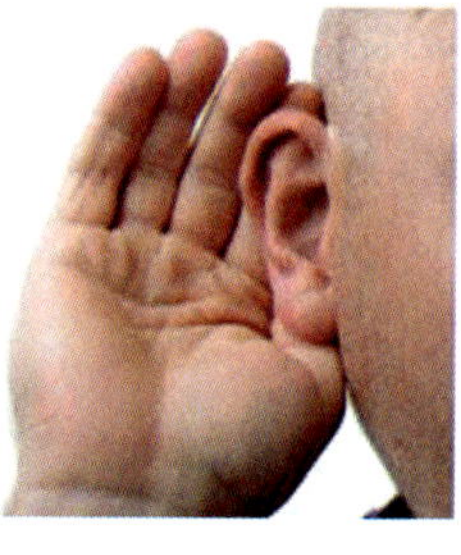

I am a Rebel

I am a rebel.

I need to socialize.

I need to share my views with Jane, Ed and Fred.

I am a Rebel

I am a rebel.

I need harmony.

I need not to care who is
white, black, and who is red.

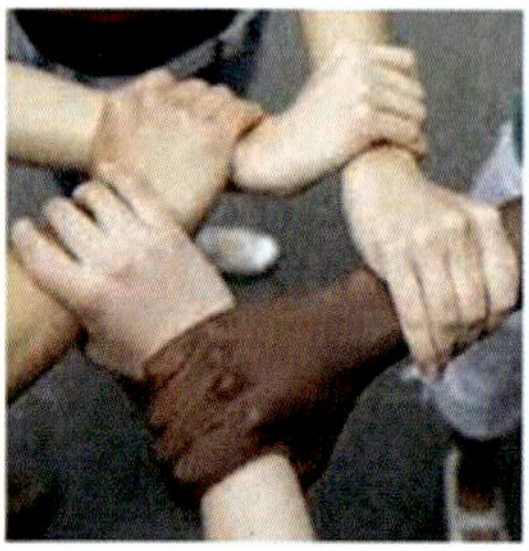

I am a Rebel

I am a rebel.

I don't need violence.

I need blood to stop from being senselessly shed.

NO VIOLENCE

I am a Rebel

I am a rebel.

I need to vote.

I need a constitution that could not be haphazardly shred.

I am a Rebel

I am a rebel.

I need security.

I need tranquility to replace all the fears and all dread.

I am a Rebel

I am a rebel.

I need information.

I need to trust the news that
I heard or just read.

I am a Rebel

I am a rebel.

I need respect.

I need you to hear me and understand what I have said.

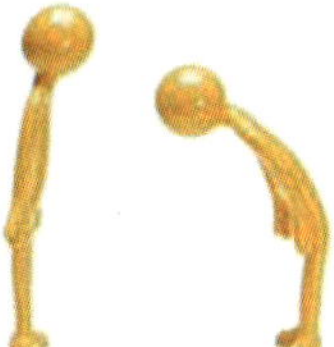

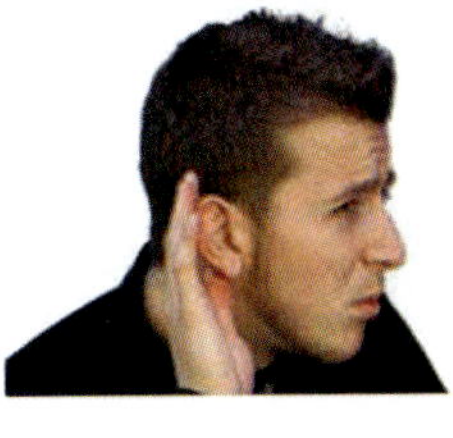

I am a Rebel

I am a rebel.

I need a megaphone.

I need this message to be sent and widely spread.

sign
protest
papers
information
diplomatic
lie

Life that is

August 21, 2013

Life is like a camera...
Focus on what's important,
Capture the good times,
Develop from the negatives,
And if things don't work out,
Take another shot.

http://www.livelifehappy.com/

Every person in this wide world comes and goes.

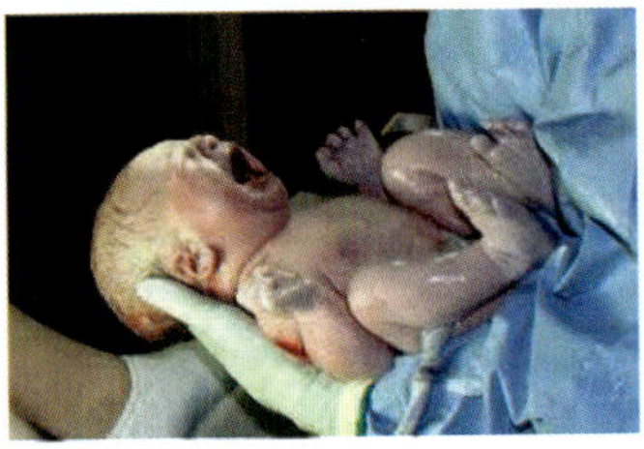

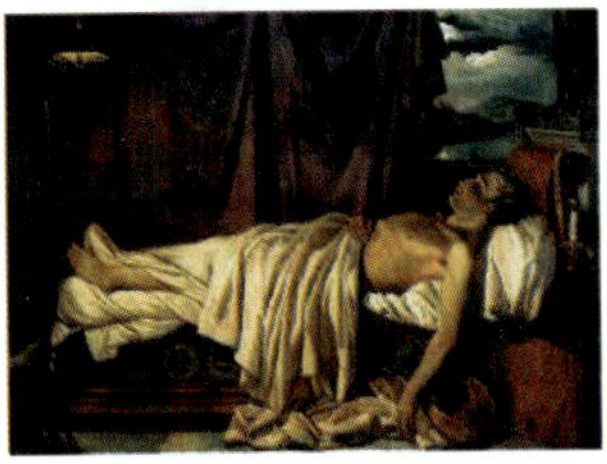

Why is he here? Why he leaves? No one knows.

Time runs unimpeded. It has no stop and no pause.

Life is random, can't tell what the days shall dispose.

Try if you will, can't alter what destiny will impose.

Be acquiescent and accepts what the times propose.

Going through life is not easy. Life has it highs and lows.

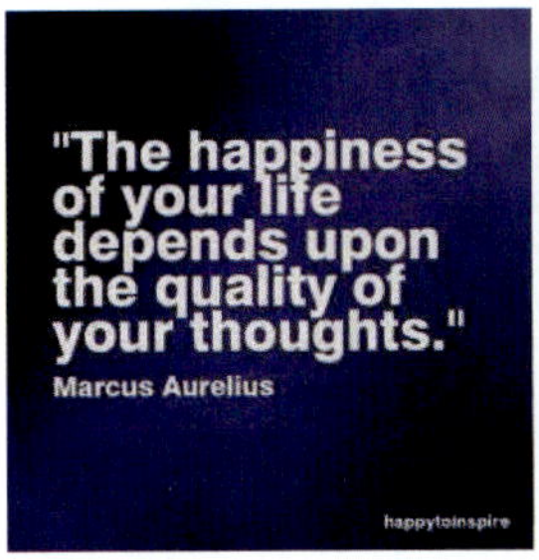

There are days where you get stones and others rose.

Bugs lurking all round you waiting to bite your toes.

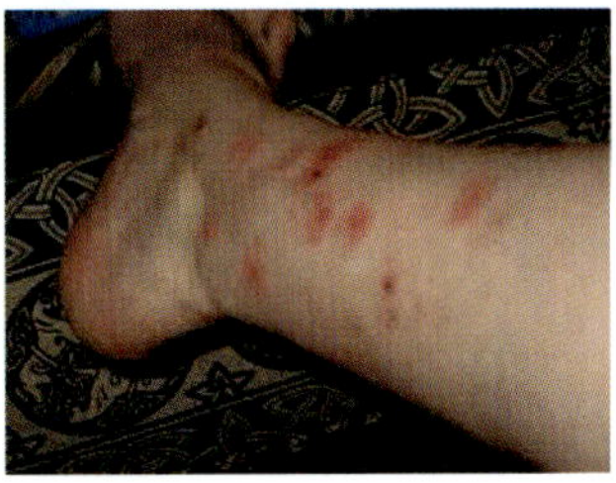

Opportunities are also abound right under your nose.

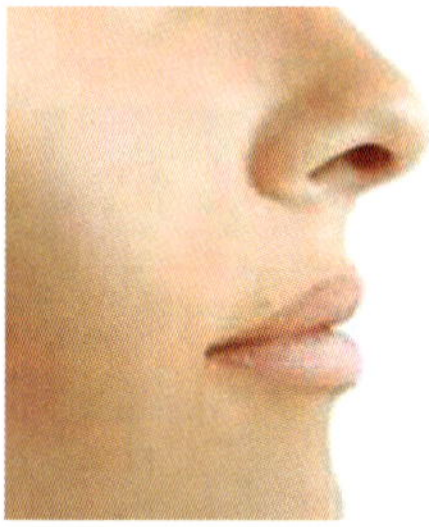

Submit to what is written and accept what life throws.

No; challenge fate and don't accept what others chose.

You need to invest in the future. Plans must compose.

Plant seed of hope. Pick the shovel and open the hose.

The tree of your struggle shall bear fruits and shows.

Optimism grows success, despair what make it slows.

Follow the righteous path. Avoid distractions or doze.

Embrace friends; watch out for the enemies and foes.

You don't need to fight obstacles with arrows and bows.

Use prudence to wide open the doors that are closed.

Mall of Life – August 5th, 2013 – Montreal Canada

Mall of Life

LIFE®

What's Life

Life is a challenge -meet it
Life is a gift -accept it
Life is a sorrow-overcome it
Life is a tragedy-face it
Life is a adventure-dare it
Life is a duty- perform it
Life is a mystery-unfold it
Life is a song -sing it
Life is a opportunity-take it
Life is a journey-complete it
Life is a promise-fulfill it
Life is a beauty-praise it
Life is a goal-achieve it
Life is a puzzle-solve it
Life is love-love it

Jessica Lee Workman

Mall of Life

LIFE®

Mall of life, what a variety of
fascinating products you offer.

You're enriched by experiences;
no one can count your coffer.

Mall of Life

LIFE®

Visiting every store, every corner,
every floor, and every aisle.

I see many types, many shapes,
many sizes, and many styles.

Mall of Life

LIFE®

In your venue, I don't look for cloths
to wear or bread to eat.

I look for beauty, flowers, birds,
and for smiles that are sweet.

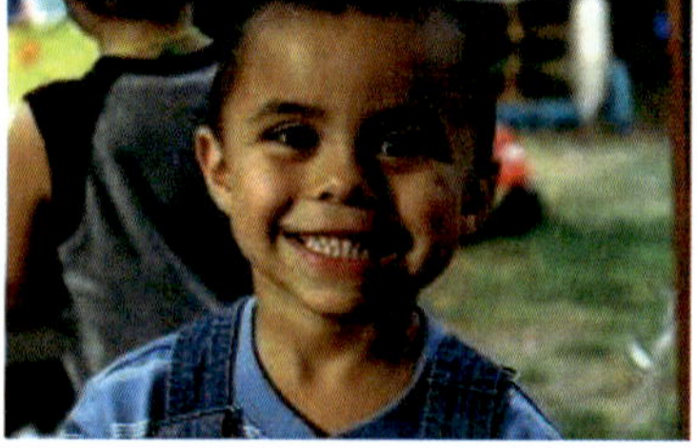

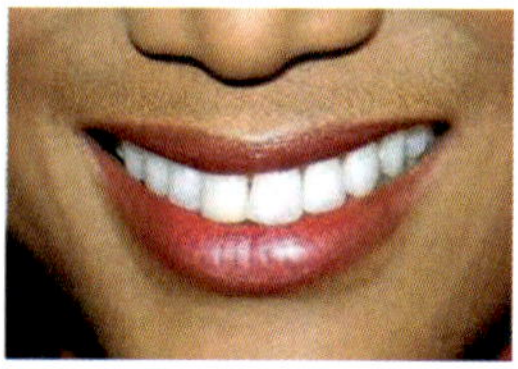

Everyone smiles in the same language

Mall of Life

LIFE®

The mall has many wonderful delicacies
that please the eyes.

Smiling babies in strollers and
toddlers running; sweet as pies.

Mall of Life

LIFE®

Different fashions and styles adorn the population's attire.

Some garish, some nice, others elegant you want to admire.

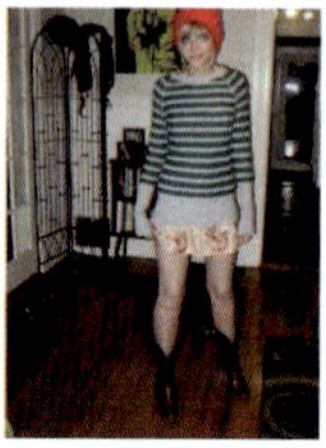

Mall of Life

LIFE®

Nothing I like more than seeing
a happy couple that is older.

Holding hands, promenading in
the mall shoulder to shoulder.

Mall of Life

LIFE®

Teenagers roaming the aisles with
friends merrily and carefree.

Like flocks of birds flying all over
and landing on a wire or a tree.

Mall of Life

LIFE®

Young and old, men and women,
singles, couples, or groups.

Passing each other, some holding
bags other licking scoops.

Mall of Life

LIFE®

I came across many products,
but this you can obviously tell.

Love is the most precious commodity
that you can't buy or sell.

LIFE
IS FULL OF
Possibilities

HEALTH
WORK
FRIENDS
CAREER
TIME
FAMILY

THE BEST
THINGS
in life are
NOT
THINGS

Mystery of a Stranger

August 4, 2013

Montreal, Canada

Let us Get To Know Each Other Better

June 12, 2009

Having the Neighbors Over for Dinner

We had the neighbors over for a dinner. One couple lives across the street and the other couple lives next to us.

We were chatting and talking about the neighborhood and the like. Then we talked about the deer population in this part of the country. My wife reported with excitements that the other day, three of them came from the neighbor's backyard into our backyard and moved on to the street. We were all pleased by the image and the event and felt it was a nice incident to cherish.

We were talking about other things and the subject of security came about. One of our neighbors informed us that lately there are break-ins in the town. Then the other neighbor's wife indicated that the other day, she saw three teenage boys coming from our neighbor's backyard through the fence and crossed our backyard to go to the street. The ladies were shocked. That is terrible, said the other wife.

I thought to myself, isn't it interesting that we like animals to cross our yard, but not humans.

Mystery of a Stranger

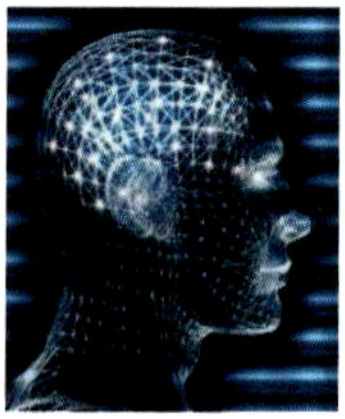

Ever wondered what is in a
person's busy head?

Wished if there were a way
a light to be shed.

Can the expression of his face
be easily read?

Glean his thoughts without
a word being said?

Mystery of a Stranger

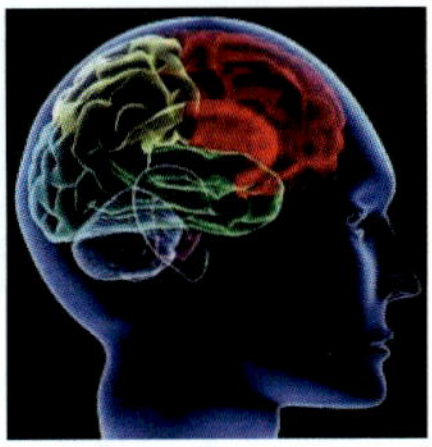

Why are we interested in the
mind of a stranger?

When he approaches us we
feel in real danger.

We immediately stiffen, this
is a game changer.

Don't know if he is a criminal
or is he a ranger.

Mystery of a Stranger

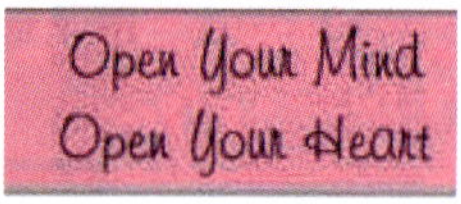

Calm down and open your
mind and your heart.

It is the logical way and
obviously being smart.

You are also a stranger to him,
let's do a restart.

Smiles do wonders, good
jester on your part.

Mystery of a Stranger

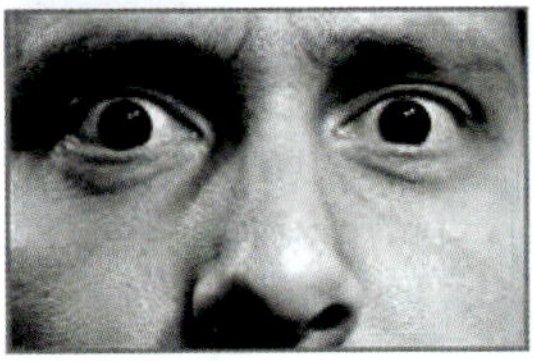

It is sad in this day and age
to fear all people.

Seeing them as reds, whites,
blacks, or purple.

It is us versus them; we're
good they're awful.

Let's agree to think of all
people being equal.

Being interested in others is
normal and natural.

It's part of our composition
being a social animal.

Our bond to each other is
quite phenomenal.

It is our greatest asset,
our ultimate collateral.

The Butterfly and the Bee

June 3, 2005

I envy the butterfly hovering around roses,
plants, and tree.

It is so beautiful, graceful, colorful,
and above all it is free.

I wish I could be just as merry, cheery,
and blithe as is she.

Hopping from a flower to a flower,
and see what it can see.

I heard a chiding; it was the disgruntled
buzzing of a bee.

I produce the honey that you enjoy;
I sweeten your morning tea.

I am the pollinator, without me, these blooms would not be.

I work without asking for favors and not even charging a fee.

How come you admire the butterfly and treat me like a flea?

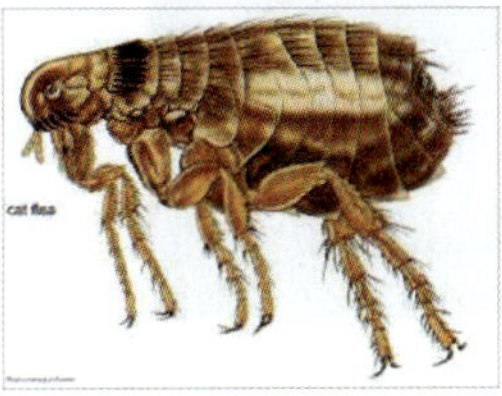

I sighed for a moment and said; you have the right scolding me.

I know about you and all the good that you bring to our society.

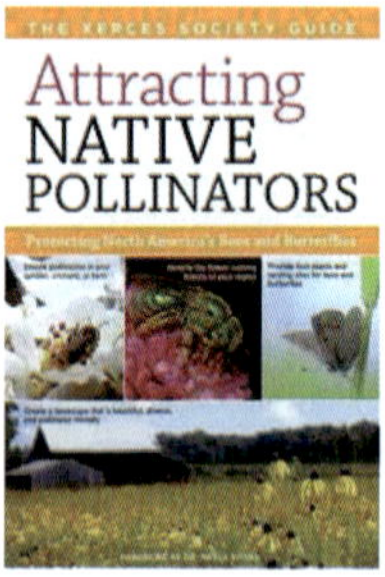

Your work ethic and your diligence are epic lessons for humanity.

© Can Stock Photo - csp13955114

Your structural skills, your societal harmony,
your lack of vanity.

The Queen Bee

These are marvelous treats that are definitely
a prized commodity.

But you see, when I notice a butterfly, I am
in awe of its royalty.

I extend the palm of my hand hoping for a
landing by her majesty.

But when I see you, I cringe, truthfully;
I really am scared of thee.

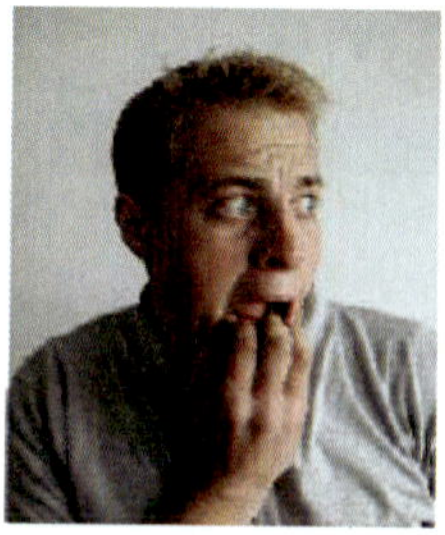

View from the Cliff

June 1, 2013

Sitting on the edge of the cliff looking
at the far horizon.
Majestic mountains, vast valleys,
view is truly amazing.
Nature is flaunting its beauty with pride,
it is quite blazon.
Here where minds and matter come
to merge and liaison.*

I enjoy the serenity of the surroundings
and the solitude.
It brings calmness to my soul and
change of attitude.
Soaring closer to the scattered clouds
on higher altitude.
Blue skies, soothing breeze, green trees,
much certitude.

I am here to seek refuge in the vastness
of here and yonder.
To give me a chance to think things over,
start to ponder.
Let go of my chains and inhibitions,
to nature I surrender.
No time restrictions, no appointment
to check on calendar.

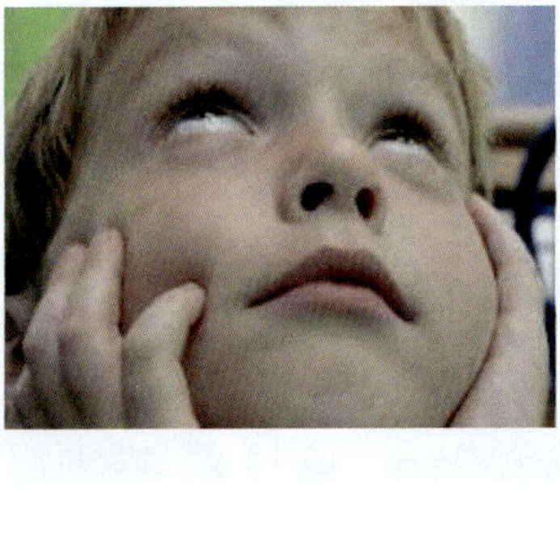

I assumed I am by myself with no worries
and no care.
Till I noticed, with many of things this
moment I share.
Life and living what tie us together
-stones, trees, and bear.
Perfect harmony that plays its tunes,
listen do not impair.

Now I began thinking of the life to
which I shall return.
Work dawn to dusk and beyond,
the bread I should earn.
Read, write, analyze, and manage,
the candles that I'll burn.
The mistakes I probably will make,
the lessons I shall learn.

My family, my friends, my neighbors
and fellow world citizens.
Dealing with colleagues, subordinates,
superiors, too partisans.
To dos, deadlines, problems to solve
challenges by the dozens.
Everyone tells the same story, busy,
juggling life like artisans.

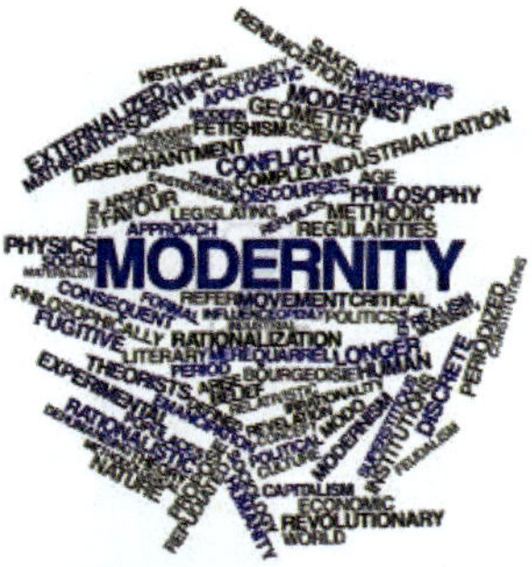

Modernity has its good and bad sides,
I must unequivocally say.
I am worried about the future, the children,
the plants, every day.
Wondering aloud why to live our lives
must nature dearly pay.
We must not harm our environment, if we
wish habitat to stay.

Bees humming, Bird chirping, lions roaring,
life is bustling.
Women caring, men working, girls singing,
boys wrestling.
Engines running, people shopping,
merchants busy hustling.
This is nature's music, the orchestra
of modern life rustling.

Clouds above should be for rain not
nuclear testing, please.
Money we spend on arms could better be
used to cure disease.
There are many of opportunities for a better
life we can seize.
Bliss is: children smiling, flowers blooming,
and a clean breeze.

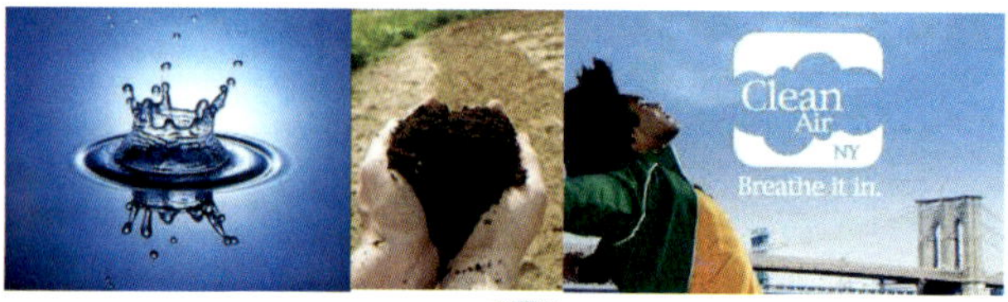

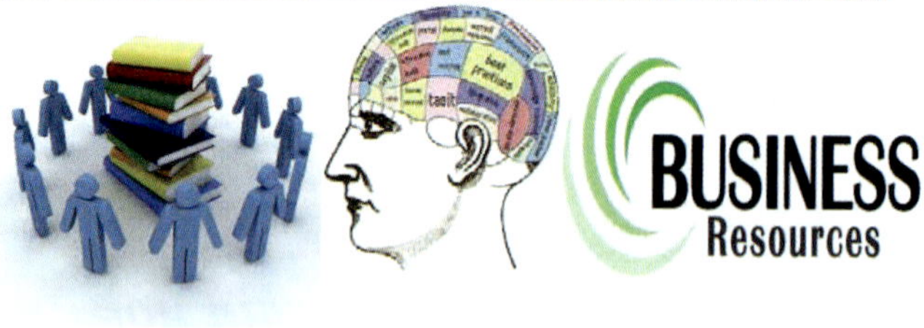

Let us do what we can to clean the water,
the soil, and the air.
Using knowledge, know how, and all the
resources we can spare.
Living in harmony and offering justice to all
it can only be fair.
Doing so, we shall pass on a better world to
our children I declare.

Save The Earth

Part B

Life in America

Arriving to America

October 8th, 1970

I Landed, I Landed

October 20, 2012

I landed, I landed.
It was magical and splendid.
Welcome message rendered.
Many papers were handed.

It was an October day.
I had arrived at JFK.
Did not know what to say.
Luckily, I made friends on my way.

I had arrived from Prague.
A stop over from Baghdad, Iraq.
Felt thrilled with a bit of shock.
My stomach clinched as a rock.

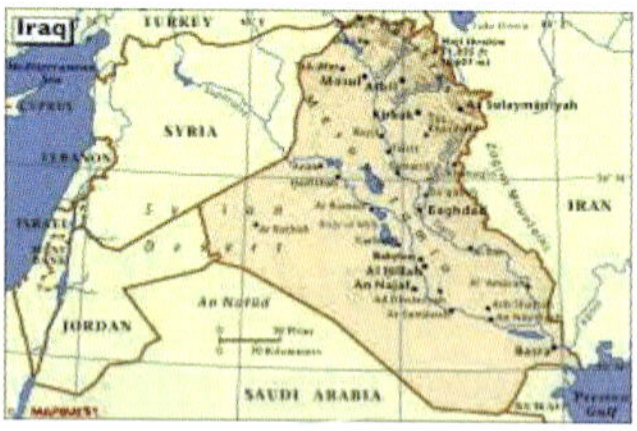

Structure the like I haven't seen.
In such a maze I haven't been.
Of the milieu I wasn't keen.
I was three years over teen.

Overwhelmed by the place.
Lugged along my suitcase.
Custom officer with smiley face.
Asked questions with grace.

I was done with the paperwork.
Ready to go to New York.
I didn't want to look like a dork.
I don't drink and I don't smoke.

Friends I met in the plane.
Helped me lodging to obtain.
It was a windy day full of rain.
Took several taxies not a train.

YMCA was our choice.
Within our budget of course.
Stay the night and rejoice.
Tomorrow see the city up close.

We were up in the high floor.
Tiny rooms with modest décor.
Shared bathrooms with no door.
Seen much worse months before.

Next morning, happy the sun did appear.
I called cousin to tell him- Hi, I am here.
His wife told me he is at work my dear.
Call in the afternoon, best news to my ear.

We had few hours to look around.
Interesting things to see were abound.
New York's attractions are renowned.
Like children in a big playground.

The city took a shower last night.
The morning was sunny and bright.
Big apple welcomed us with delight.
Ready to explore and see few sights.

Uptown we walked from thirty four.
Time Square we wanted to explore.
Navigating through the crowd was a chore.
Everything was big, tall buildings I adore.

I remembered when I was young.
Going to America was on my tongue.
Dreaming to breathe its air in my lung.
Absorb its culture and sing its song.

Well, we were in Time Square.
Nothing to it could compare.
Thousands milling and no stare.
Like a big theatre with no chair.

Vendors selling this and that.
People wearing strange hat.
Short and tall, skinny and fat.
No one cared where you sat.

People were doing their thing.
Some dancing and others sing.
Memory of childhood those bring.
It was autumn, felt like spring.

The year was nineteen seventy.
The going-on in the world was plenty.
Visiting the UN Site seemed nifty.
It was a Saturday, the offices empty.

Said goodbye to the friends and took a taxi.
Alone not knowing the town seemed risky.
But the driver put me at ease was frisky.
Arrived at the bus station terminal musky.

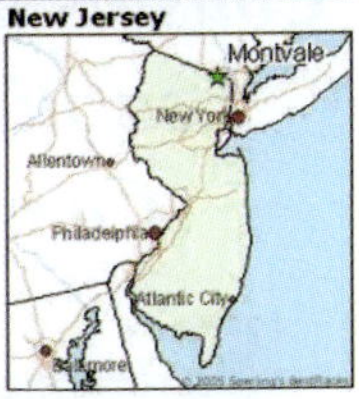

Got ticket to where my cousin was.
Didn't know how many stops it has.
Arrived at my destination with my jazz.
Of my accent no one made a razz.

Cousins picked me to their home.
Large house with space to roam.
Baths to bathe, brush, and comb.
Dinette area shaped liked a dome.

I was a lost fish looking for a pool.
Cousins helped me with my school.
Learning the language was very cool.
Commuting back and forth was cruel.

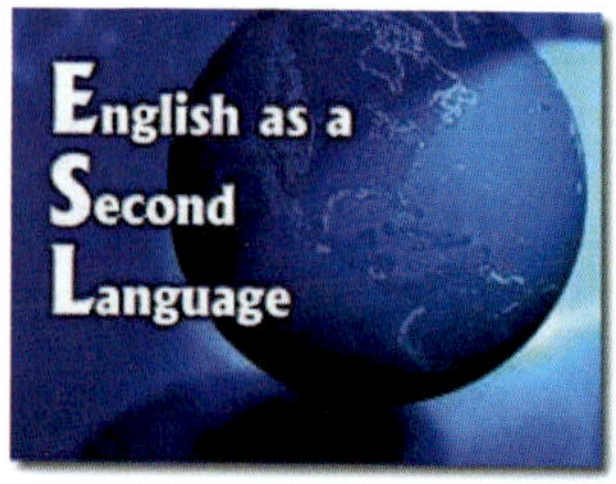

I needed to find my own place.
That was the start of what I'll face.
Started the journey joined the race.
Looked forward to challenges to embrace.

I left cousins' home in few weeks.
Independence and self-reliance I seek.
I was studious, you may say a geek.
My performance was at its peak.

I found a room near the school I attend.
The landlady was a mother and godsend.
Tenants were great and became my friend.
The rent was close to what I could spend.

In few days, I found a job in Shop Rite.
I was set. Felt everything is going alright.
I was going to achieve my goals and sight.
The land of opportunity has done me right.

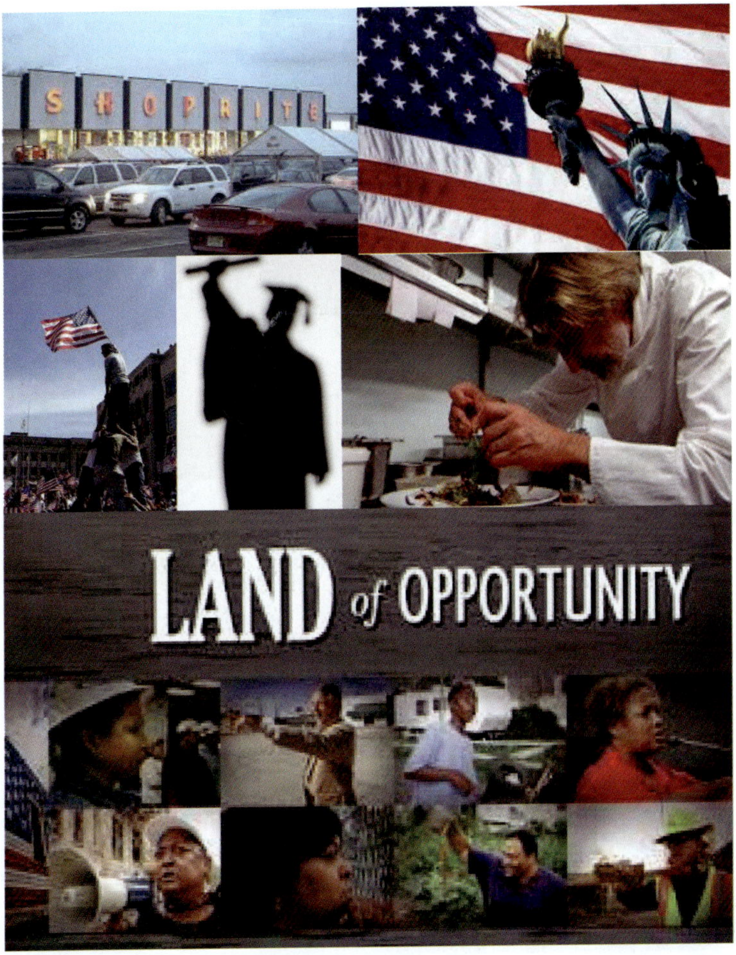

America, My Home

September 21, 2013

America, will you love me as much
as I love you with no hesitation?
Will you protect me as I swore
to protect you without vacillation?
Will you value me as I value your
constitution, laws, and regulations?
Will you respect me as I respect
your system, structure, institutions?
Will you embrace me as I embraced
your culture with fascination?
Will you take me in as a productive
member of your noble population?

Will you respect who I am, where
I come from, and what I cleave?
Will you love me regardless of my
gender, color, shape, or believe?
Will you give me the opportunity
to set goals and work to achieve?
Will you provide me with the best
education that I could receive?
Will you allow me to pursue any
career I wish to engage in or perceive?
Will you let me go anywhere I want
to go, free to come or to leave?

Will you let me engage in business and
help me along in my endeavor?
Will you let me take advantage of the
best technological advances ever?
Will you cover me with the finest
healthcare that is possible forever?
Will you let me enjoy the best of
musicians and artisans who are clever?
Will you let me aspire to go to
Venus, Mercury, and Mars, whichever?
Will you let me be who I want to be
without restrictions whatsoever?

Will you let me participate freely in
the political process and petition?
Will you let me elect my own local and
national leaders for any position?
Will you let me express my opinions
without reservation, fear, or suspicion?
Will you allow me to know what going
on without a need for permission?
Will you let me associate with anyone
I want without prior admission?
Will you allow me to serve my country
freely and without any condition?

America answered yes to all the
questions asked with a bit of quiver.
Did it always fulfill all these promises
to all the people, perhaps never?
If you review its performance over its
history, in disgust you'll shiver.
Working to redeem itself; changing its
course and trying to do better.
Much has been done since its inception;
many evidences you discover.
Despite all its ills, I unequivocally say
America is the best nation ever.

IF YOU DON'T LIKE IT HERE

GO HOME!

September 27, 2013

IF YOU DON'T LIKE IT HERE

GO HOME!

During the second Iraq War, we used to have heated political discussion.

This we used to do with my colleagues during our lunch sessions.

I am from Iraq, a victim of Saddam's ruthless and ugly oppression.

I was grateful to America, ridding Iraq of this regime, my confession.

IF YOU DON'T LIKE IT HERE

GO HOME!

However, I questioned America's real motive and disagreed with many policy positions.

I argued my points with facts and figures with engineering precision.

I apparently irked one of my colleagues, he shouted "If you don't like it here, go home"; So, I looked for remission.

IF YOU DON'T LIKE IT HERE

GO HOME!

I came here of my own volition.

I worked hard to educate myself.
I paid for my own tuition.

I followed the rules. I gained legal admission.

I learned about this country's history, its system, its culture, and followed its progression.

IF YOU DON'T LIKE IT HERE

GO HOME!

I abided by its laws and regulations.
I admired its constitution.
I declared my submission.

I lived with its people. I love what the
country stands for and its
mission.

I became a naturalized citizen.
A dream came to fruition.

I chose to be a citizen. I went through
the process. It was my decision.

IF YOU DON'T LIKE IT HERE

GO HOME!

Unlike you, who is citizen because
of accident of birth,
I needed permission.

That entitles me to speak freely,
question my government's policies,
criticize misguided wars,
and talk against rendition.

I came from a different land, a different
culture; I might be able to contribute
positively to my adopted
country by sharing my vision.

IF YOU DON'T LIKE IT HERE

GO HOME!

I love this country. It is my home. I want to participate in the dialogue, if I question or criticize, that does not mean derision.

I want my country to be the best that it could be, one way to do that is to point out its errors and omissions.

Part C

America Today

The State of the Nation

September 25, 2013

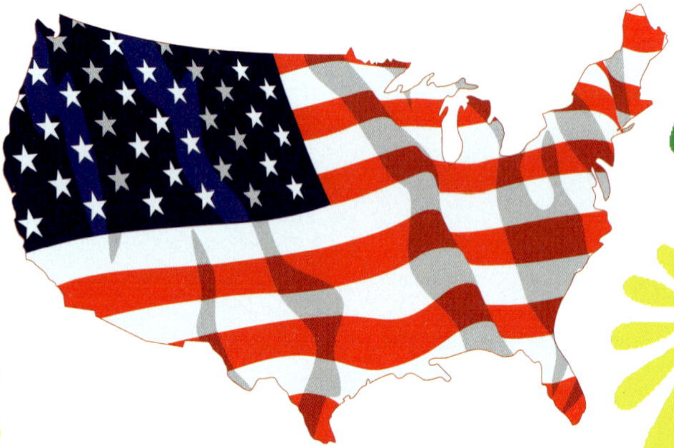

The State of the Nation

America always wants to do what is right
and what is absolutely the best.

Unfortunately, today, it acts as a lost soul
and the devil has occupied its chest.

Politicians act for their own narrow interest
saying the hell with the rest.

Lobbyists rule the country; money controls
what agenda to manifest.

Ethic is missing from the conduct of the
politicians we elected with zest.

Partisan politics is the order of the day;
class warfare is sadly in a crest.

The State of the Nation

The country faces many problems that need
solutions; that is for sure.

Mass murders, bankruptcies, foreclosures,
and illnesses in need of cure.

Political wrangling, Governmental disarray,
and many crisis de jour.

There are few people who are rich and
millions more who are poor.

Many people live in slums while others busy
sailing or are on a tour.

A situation that is not fair and can no longer
be accepted or endure.

The State of the Nation

Let us look at the media and its tilted
delivery and biased news crafting.

There are millions of issues that could be
talked about as of this writing.

Some of them are mundane, some
important, and others are very exciting.

Bulletin of the day maybe Government
Shutdown or an illegal dogfighting.

Which celebrity is divorcing, who is dating
whom, or their beach sighting.

Political news is never without opinion.
Finding the fact is very daunting.

The State of the Nation

Integrity is waning in our conduct; ethic is
bowing to the mighty dollar.

We don't care about the poor, the hungry,
and those living in squalor.

We love music, sports, cars, restaurants,
and visiting the beauty parlor.

We value those who entertain us more than
a professor and a scholar.

We skirt the law, our chances of getting
caught is getting much smaller.

We point out other people's shortcomings;
we see our actions much taller.

The State of the Nation

We spend billions on armaments without
hesitation or the slightest concern.

Hardware acquired not to defend the country,
but to elect him for another turn.

Meanwhile, he adamantly opposes any money
spent to help children learn.

Offering no money for infrastructure or
research, so the economy could churn.

Advocating tax relief for the rich. Cut
spending;
we don't have money to burn.

Government is too big. Make it smaller. It
spends much more than it could earn.

The State of the Nation

There is truth in what is being said.
Government is a bloated bureaucracy.

Denying this fact is definitely short sighted
and is the ultimate in hypocrisy.

Too many redundancies and overlapping
policies that weakens democracy.

Unlike a business; staffing and promotions
is not based on meritocracy.

People working for the Government think
they are members of aristocracy.

Government is there to serve the people;
it should not act as an autocracy.

The State of the Nation

Unions were a blessing for the hardworking
laborers that needed a voice.

Employees worked under conditions that were
harsh they had no choice.

Unions, through bargaining, extracted rights
for the laborers to rejoice.

But, things went too far. Now, unions act
much like a military force.

Unions' unreasonable demands cripple
the businesses function of course.

Contentious relations between management
and labor are getting worse.

The State of the Nation

Traditional farming has given way to
mega-farming that is quite lean.

Less than one percent is engaged in the
business of farming as seen.

We import much of our fruits, vegetables,
and all sort of dry beans.

Farm corporations make billions in profits;
subsidies we must wean.

They cry foul, we need subsides, to the
agribusiness you are being mean.

Politicians seeking farmers' votes, for changing
this policy are not so keen.

The State of the Nation

Our education has suffered setbacks and is
falling year by year.

Blame it on policies, lack of funding, and the
unions my dear.

You cannot question teachers; they are angels
you can't smear.

Dilapidated school structures impede learning
and induce fear.

Overcrowded classes overwhelm the teacher,
which is quite clear.

Salute the dedicated teachers who need help
for the students to steer.

The State of the Nation

The cost of healthcare skyrocketing for many
reasons day by day.

Corrupt insurance and pharmaceutical
companies practices at play.

They have the money to lobby politicians for
the status quo to stay.

Average citizens are stuck with the bill; they
have not much to say.

Paying more for healthcare causes plans for
other programs to fray.

Our healthcare system is convoluted and
burdensome; I must say.

The State of the Nation

Many guns all around us, killing and shooting
is the dominant trend.

Every day, children, men, and women dying
by guns; this is the wend.

Curtailing ownership of military style high
caliber guns they fend.

Current limit on magazine capacity, this law
they do not wish to bend.

Proponent of unrestricted gun ownership
have money and the upper hand.

We shall see more children's funerals; which
politicians ready to attend.

The State of the Nation

Drug abuse, alcoholism, and smoking are
quite prevalent in our society.

Finding someone without one of these
afflictions is rare and an oddity.

We don't spend money to educate and
prevent this horrible impropriety.

The economic effect of these problems are
great and cause national anxiety.

Our prisons are filled with drug dealers
and abusers with regularity.

Money better spent on rehabilitation,
educate, and give them parity.

The State of the Nation

Our offspring are a lost generation that in
need of guidance and direction.

They spend more time on gaming, sport,
and TV, that's quite an addiction.

They are sinking deep in materialism; they
have many options for selection.

The violent games they play; lure them to
do more; a very bad affliction.

The shows the children watch or games
they play have violent depiction.

Saying that these games are harmless; is a
real fallacy and pure fiction.

The State of the Nation

A sizeable number of our fellow citizens are
incarcerated.

They live in correctional facilities that
are privately operated.

The reasons vary, so do the length of time
they are separated.

Invest in the children from the start and
help them better situated.

Use the money to jail people to give them
skills and make them educated.

No matter what we do, crimes could not
be stopped or eradicated.

The State of the Nation

Sadly, we have a very litigious society
indeed.

This person suing that person every day
you read.

Law makers create laws to plant this
frenzy's seed.

I ask why is it that we have so many
lawyers to feed.

In other countries, they have fewer and
they proceed.

Having too many lawyer causes our
economy to bleed.

Big Business in America

October 18, 2013

Big Business in America

Minimum wage is eight dollars per hour,
for unskilled blue-collar.
We must make this number much smaller.
Rich businessmen holler.
We can run our operations abroad,
paying a dime for each dollar.
You want us to create jobs her in America?
An act of extreme valor.
We need cheap labor. We're not
looking for exceptional scholar.

Big Business in America

Considering the difference, we should
most domestic laborers fire.
No labor laws and no benefits,
foreign laborers we should hire.
Labor choices are many. We get the
same talent as we did prior.
The same work done with much lower
rate for any job we desire.
This is the Global Economy, don't
sweat it, and don't perspire.

Big Business in America

Modernizing, we automate and use
robots to run production.
Speed operation, enhance precision,
and get labor reduction.
Robots don't tire and don't require
care, attain perfection.
But they can't do all what humans
can do, that is a fiction.
For that reason, we still need
positions run by human diction.

Big Business in America

Gone those days where employees were
treasured, ideas from times older.
Our goal is to make money and create value
for ourselves and our shareholder.
A noble goal that drives our policies and
written in our constitutional folder.
Shareholders trust our management decisions
and approve our work order.
We act in our self-interest; there is a big
responsibility on all our shoulder.

Big Business in America

Silly times of enticing talent to work for us
by offering perks are gone.
We play the games of merger and acquisition,
the employees are the pawn.
Commitment to the employees' future
and well beings we have none.
Their welfare should be subservient to
keeping the company financially brawn.
Employees are just IDs and numbers; don't
know Harriet, Peter, or John.

Big Business in America

We want to advance our goals. We are not
responsible for our community.
We can't worry about the environment.
We can act with total impunity.
We can buy politicians to make laws that
suit us and give us immunity.
We hate paying taxes, rules, and regulations;
we speak it loud in unity.
If the government needs money, let it
raid Medicare and social security.

Big Business in America

The big boys in the corporate boardroom
get the big fat check.
No matter how they damage the company
and lives they wreck?
Productive employees who do the work
are slashed by the neck.
In times of trouble, hundred lose their
positions to clear the deck.
But management increases its bonuses
and benefits, what the heck?

Big Business in America

On your commitment for the good of the
country you must be strongly chided.
Looking from the long-term view; this
approach is extremely short-sighted.
Should businesses be exempt
from responsibilities? On this
the nation is divided.
You're shooting the hand that is feeding you.
There is no way you can hide it.
Turning your back on your employees,
your consumers, is totally misguided.

Big Business in America

Using foreign laborers and introduction of
technology, we can understand.
The people, that being furloughed by these
practices, need a helping hand.
Proper training must be provided for the
skills that the industries demand.
Investing in infrastructure and research
what make us strong and grand.
Working together for a better future for
our children, a plot must be planned.

Big Business in America

To build the home of our nation's future we
need a strong and solid foundation.
We should work together rich and poor as
one body that makes up our nation.
Political bickering and government paralysis
causes bad economic stagnation.
The nation needs to invest in infrastructure,
research, and profound education.
To achieve this goal we need help from
government and business
participation.

Shame On Us

November 2, 2013

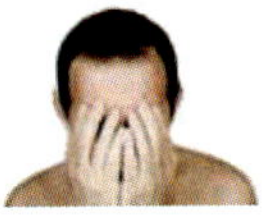

Shame On Us

Shame on us for our lack of concern
for humanity.
Shame on us for not giving our
environment priority.
Shame on us for not advancing
equality and parity.
Shame on us for our lack of kindness
and charity.
Shame on us for our lack of goodwill
and its rarity.
Shame on us for all the conflicts
and our insanity.
Shame on us for all our selfishness
and ugly vanity.
Shame on us for our lack of decorum
and profanity.
Shame on us for confusing talk
and lack of clarity.
Shame on us for our greed
and robbing our posterity.

Shame On Us

Shame on us for all the senseless wars
and its barbarity.
Shame on us for our apathy
and lack of solidarity.
Shame on us for our corrupt politic
and its polarity.
Shame on us for promoting hate,
wiping out hilarity.
Shame on us for our ignorance
and lack of familiarity.
Shame on us for our abnormal
behaviors and peculiarity.
Shame on us for our phony friendship
and lack of sincerity.
Shame on us for imposing our way
and our temerity.
Shame on us for our lack of
organization and irregularity.
Shame on us for our wasteful ways
that kills trees and manatee.

EPS10 SAMPLETEXT

Healthcare

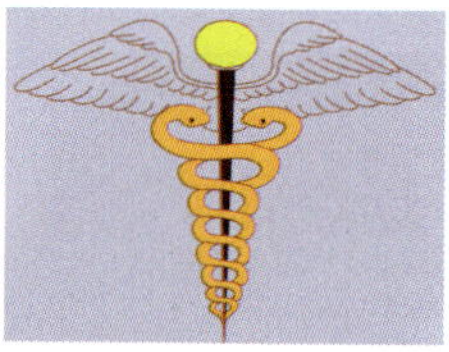

November 16, 2013

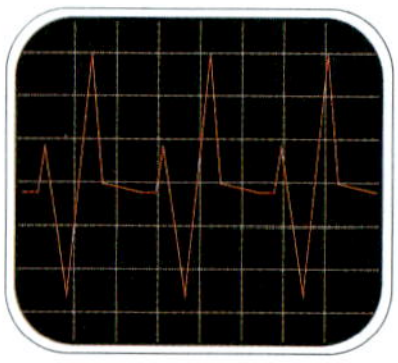

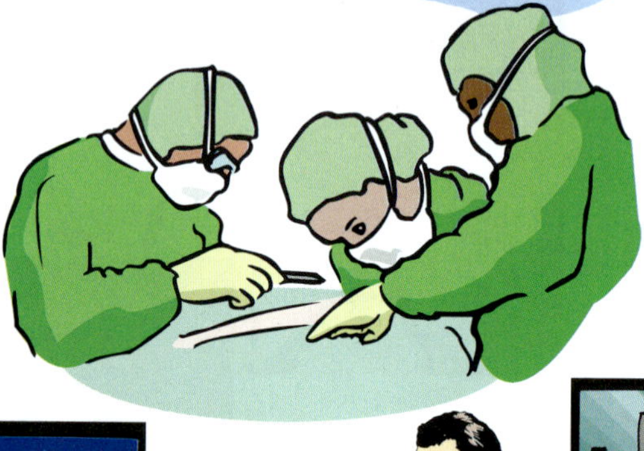

Healthcare

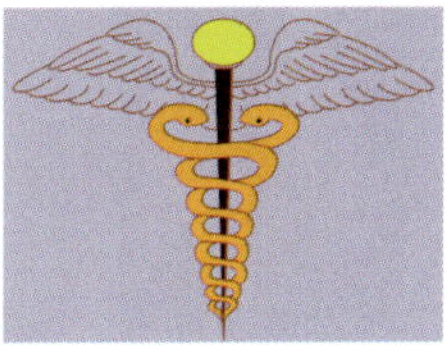

Yes, yes; I believe in the universal coverage
for healthcare.

I strongly believe all citizens should be
covered by Medicare.

Why should businesses the cost of healthcare
coverage bear.

Let the Government cover the cost; that's
only logical and fair.

To call it a form of socialism, you should
not think of it or dare.

Healthcare

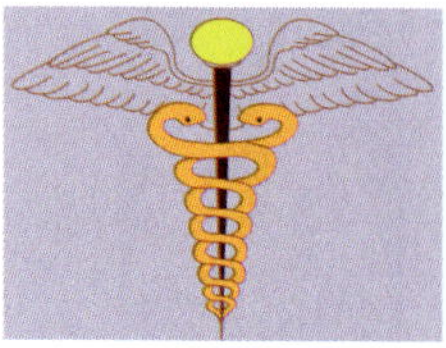

We pay for defense; security is government
responsibility to care.

Individuals don't have to buy armaments to
fend the land and the air.

What is the difference between viruses
and humans in warfare?

They are all enemies intend to do us harm;
of that you're aware.

We should offer a uniform solution that
serves us all; I declare.

Healthcare

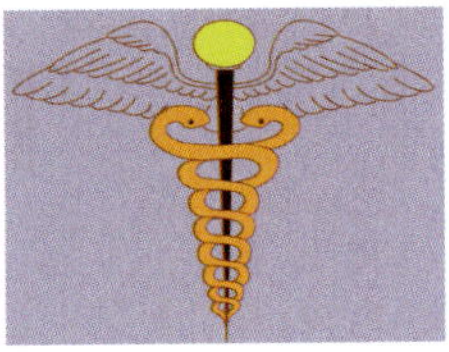

We'll rid ourselves from fraud and the big
national nightmare.

We reduce the load on physicians and the
paperwork flare.

Malpractice adds to the medical office
burden a large share.

Let us put a limit on lawsuits. Stop lawyers
feeding in the lair.

Keep the doctors attend to the patients'
needs; remove the legal scare.

The Gun Debate

December 18, 2012

The Gun Debate

http://en.wikipedia.org/wiki/Sandy_Hook_massacre#Gun_control

In his speech at the December 16 vigil, Obama called for using "whatever power this office holds", to prevent similar tragedies in the future. Within 15 hours of the incident, 100,000 Americans signed a petition at the Obama administration's We the People petitioning website in support of a renewed national debate on gun control. President Obama later affirmed that he would make gun control a "central issue" at the start of his second term of office, in a speech on December 19; signing 23 executive orders and proposing 12 congressional actions regarding gun control, one month after the shooting. The President formed a Gun Violence Task Force to be led by Vice President Joe Biden to address the causes of gun violence in the United States. Senators Dianne Feinstein and Joe Lieberman called for an assault weapon ban, with Feinstein intending to introduce a ban bill on the first day of the new Congress, while former Congresswoman Gabrielle Gifford, who was shot and injured in a 2011 shooting in Tucson, has launched Americans for Responsible Solutions to raise money for further gun control efforts in light of the Sandy Hook shooting. Fear of future restrictions on firearms led to a spike in sales of guns, ammunition, and magazines in the weeks following the shooting.

On December 21, 2012, the National Rifle Association called on the United States Congress to appropriate funds for the hiring of armed police officers in every American school to protect students. The NRA also announced the creation of a school protection program called the National School Shield Program, which would be led by former Drug Enforcement Administration (DEA) administrator and United States Congressman Asa Hutchinson.

more

The Gun Debate

http://en.wikipedia.org/wiki/Sandy_Hook_massacre#Gun_control

A month after the shooting, President Obama cited the incident while announcing proposals for increased gun control. His proposals included universal background checks on firearms purchases, an assault weapons ban, and limiting magazine capacity to 10 cartridges. Relatives of the victims in the shooting and survivors from other mass shootings were official guests during the announcement.
On January 17, 2013, the Utah Sheriffs' Association sent a letter to President Obama criticizing attempts "to demonize firearms". In the letter, they suggested that they would refuse to uphold federal laws that restricted the Second Amendment rights of their constituents.
In reaction to anticipated restrictions on firearms, gun permit applications increased dramatically in a multi-state trend that followed the Connecticut school shooting.
On April 17, 2013, a bill that would have seen the restrictions on gun control, known as the Minchin-Toomey Background Checks Bill, failed to pass the U.S. Senate by six votes, with 48 democrats and 4 Republicans voting for the bill, and 5 democrats and 41 Republicans voting against. The NRA released a statement critiquing the bill, stating that "expanding background checks, at gun shows or elsewhere, will not reduce violent crime or keep our kids safe in their schools." In a speech the following day, Obama called the failing of the bill "shameful" and stated how the Republicans had "willfully lied" about the proposal on background checks, while Ted Cruz, a leading opponent of the bill, stated that making a registry is the only way to make the background checks effective.

End

NRA says guns are part of our constitution,
should not be smeared.
They are used for our protection and hunting
and not to be feared.
The politicians that tow our line must be
supported and cheered.
So, anyone who wants to have multiple guns
should not be jeered.
Arms in the hands of people keeps the government
from being veered.
It is a tool to make sure people rights are
protected and not veneered.
Never mind the thousands who are killed
every year, guns are cleared.
People kill people, guns are not to be blamed
or even be sneered.
Innocent children dying is the price we must
pay, the NRA decreed.
Our right to hold gun is above all other
rights and must be revered.

You who representing us from Miami,
Phoenix, or Dearborn.
I ask you to tell the truth with no intent to
demean or much scorn.
You want to protect a fetus in his mother's
womb not yet born.
But don't care much about him alive, I'm
saddened and forlorn.
Claiming to be prolife; a wrong sound coming
from a bad horn.
Passion for the sick, the poor, or the needy is
definitely not shown.
However, to uphold the interest of the privileged
you are forsworn.
But guns have nothing to do with being rich or
poor, why the torn.
Bullets don't distinguish cotton or silk when
piercing a body's loin.
Please think of the people's safety, not who
pays to mow your lawn.

This part of my message is for the NRA to
understand and hear.
Upholding the second amendment is primary,
let others sear.
You value your freedom; the authority causes
you much fear.
You claim you need guns so that government
could not interfere.
You cannot fight tanks and missiles with rifles,
let us be clear.
You have right to vote, that is the weapon, not a
gun or a spear.
You want to hunt, why do you need a machinegun
to kill a deer?
Your insistence on carrying guns engenders
images of yesteryear.
People roamed in vast lands their need for
protection was sincere.
Today, we live in civil societies; there is no need
for guns, dear.

 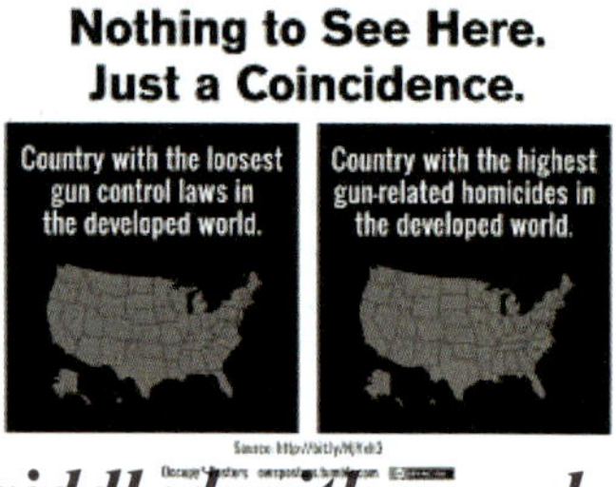

Images of children's bodies riddled with gunshots
disturbs us all.
We need to protect these precious innocent jewels
large or small.
No more students lolling dead in the classrooms
around the hall.
Stop lunatics from having powerful guns killing
boys playing ball.
Fearing shooters, girls should not hide under the
table or the stall.
People scared to enter cinemas, go to parks, or
shop at the mall.
Many people are dying by guns, worse time than
this I can't recall.
Lives are cut short; don't see winter, spring,
summer or the fall.
Ask congress to enact laws to secure us, don't
delay or forestall.
Stopping guns from the hands of unauthorized
should be the goal.

Patriot

July 19, 2013

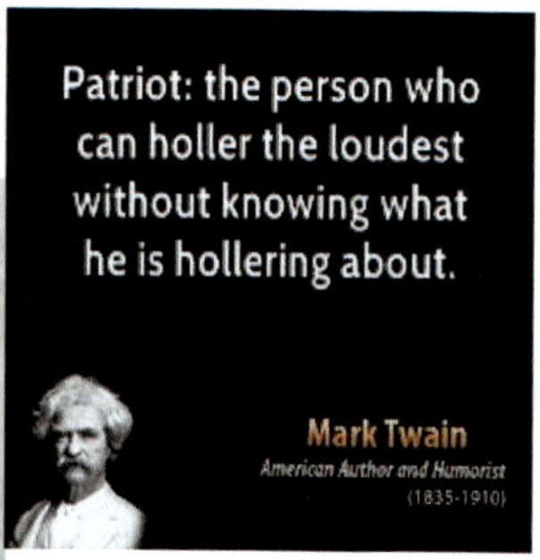

Patriots

July 19, 2013

There are two kinds of patriots -those who claim to be one and those who really are.

- *The first kind believes that he must have all the privileges and the country must serve him.*
- *The other kind believes it is a privilege to serve the country.*

- *The first kind will love the country so long it supports his interest to accumulate wealth or pursue a narrow agenda.*
- *The other kind will give his life to support the interest of the country.*

- *The first kind expects the majority to forfeit its share to increase his own minority interest.*
- *The other kind will forfeit his interest for the good of the majority.*

- *The first kind uses his financial and organizational power to manipulate public perceptions and to influence politicians to advance his agenda.*
- *The other kind grows hapless, day by day, and finds himself powerless to prevent the country from declining.*

Continues

Patriots

July 19, 2013

My message to the real patriot is to unite. Be aware of what is going on in the world around you. Do not let sleek special interest group and the politicians fool you. One tactic the special interest group use, to advance their agenda, is: merging their issues (interest) with other legitimate issues.

In recent years, we see the country is split into two camps -right (conservative) and left (liberal). Each camp bundles some social issues with other economic or fiscal issues. Example: conservatives use the emotional abortion, gun, and immigration issues to garnish votes for their candidates. They perhaps may not be interested in these issues, as such, but they use them to win seats for their candidates. Their hope is that their candidates will advance their interest for smaller government, lower taxes, and less regulations. On the other hand, liberals also use these same issues to advance their own agenda in the same manner as the conservatives. They hope, their candidates will support bigger government, more taxes (mainly from the rich), and more regulations. You as a patriot must be alert and make sure that you separate these issues. Why can you not be fiscally liberal on some issues and socially conservative on some other issues? Why can we not address each issue by itself outside of a label? Perhaps this is hard to do today because of the two-party system we have.

End

4TH OF JULY
GOD
BLESS
AMERICA
LAND OF THE FREE
HOME OF THE BRAVE

Tell me, what is the difference?

June 13, 2013

Tell me, what is the difference?

There are exceptions to all the rules,
good politicians with fortitude.

Noble servants dedicating their lives
to serve the people with rectitude.

You are the few who carry the flag,
you have our utmost gratitude .

You the politician, who declare aloud
with much fanfare and certitude.

I will do my best for the people,
not the privileged few but the multitude.

I promise that I will serve my constituents
with the highest exactitude.

Bad
Politicians
Are Elected by
Good People Who
Don't Vote

Alas, when you secure the position,
you change your prior attitude.

You become partisan -to your party's agenda
you become solidly glued.

Follow special interest issues,
people's matters you always seclude.

You sell your soul to the highest bidder
and become really crude.

Work to push lobbyists' agenda,
nation's interest you will exclude.

You waste public money,
your judgment become very much skewed.

The plans, prior to your election,
have been by your masters brewed.

You are a puppet, your strings are pulled
and your words are cued.

On the inside you are conniving,
outside you are proper and prude.

You are focused on what is good for you.
A mindset cannot be slued.

As a result of your inactions,
the country is derailing, troubles ensued.

You do what your bosses ask you;
don't care much for public mood.

*This definitely cannot be questioned
or ignored or logically argued.*

*People need jobs, homes, healthcare,
security, clean air and safe food.*

*Your agenda does not match what
the people want. Wake up, dude.*

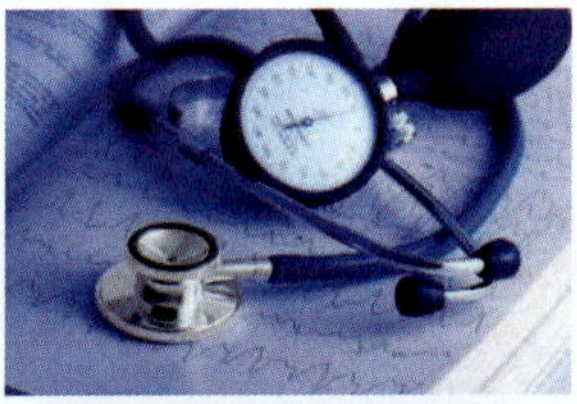

At the end, there is only one thing
I can absolutely positively conclude.

When your promises and actions
are examined and thoroughly reviewed.

There is not much difference between
you and a regular cheap prostitute.

homeless
jobless

Democracy & Justice

July 15, 2013

DEMOCRACY

OF THE PEOPLE BY THE PEOPLE FOR THE PEOPLE

JUSTICE

Judicial System in a Democracy

I was in London on October 3rd, 1995, working with an American and British team on a major communications project for XYZ Communications, UK (not the real name). At that time, much of the American Media, and to some extent, the British media were extensively covering the O. J. Simpson's trial gavel to gavel. O. J. Simpson was accused of killing his ex-wife, Nicole Brown, and her companion, Ronald Goldman. Mr. Simpson is black and a football hero. The victims were white. The jury was composed of 8 women and four men. Eight of the jurors were black, two Hispanic, and two of mixed race.

That day, it was announced that the Jury had reached a verdict and the Judge would ask the jury to come to court and give their decision. It was late at night in London and the afternoon in California. We all gathered in one of my American colleagues' house to watch the verdict live. Most of us were one hundred percent sure that the verdict would be guilty. It must be noted that all of us were white. Some of the American were from the south. While waiting for the verdict, one of the southern colleagues, went on at length extolling the capabilities of the lead attorney for the prosecutor-Marcia Clark. He declared, "I would not want to be in front of her in a court. She is one tough cookie.". Well, when the verdict was announced and O. J. Simpson was found not guilty, we all were surprised, and the juices were drained from us. We were extremely disappointed and felt that justice was not served.

continued

In the summer of 2013, the country was also hooked on the trial of George Zimmerman, a white man, accused of shooting Trayvon Martin to death . Trayvon was an unarmed 17-year-old black boy. The jury was composed of six women, five white and one minority. In this case the jury also found the accused not guilty and acquitted Mr. Zimmerman. Here also, I felt that justice was not served.

If one looks at these two cases, it seems it is a tit for tat case. You let a black murderer go free, we will let a white murderer go free. But I really don't think that what happened. The fact is simply that jurors don't have the expertise to judge such complicated cases. They are easily manipulated by highly paid high-powered lawyers. The proof of this is that Mr. Simpson was found guilty by a different jury in a subsequent civil suit. In the case of Mr. Zimmerman, the justice Department may consider a civil rights violation suit. Thus, I declare that the Jury System, despite it being glorified as a tool of democracy, must be abandoned. How can we let several lay people determine the guilt or innocence of an accused? They don't have the training, the expertise, the knowledge of the law to be able to decide such matters. That why, the judge has to instruct them what to consider and how to evaluate the case. The jury, composed of average citizens, is no substitute for knowledgeable judges and lawyers. You may say, but that is in our constitution. My response is that we are misinterpreting the intent of the framers. They wanted cases to be judged by judges who come from the same stock as the accused, and not from upper level of the society.

Democracy says,
majority rules not the selected few.

What one half plus one decides,
the rest should do.

Votes are counted by absolute numbers,
not by who.

Not by knowledge, not by wealth,
not by size of shoe.

Matters not, tall, short, skinny or fat,
Robert, Mary, or Hugh.

Not a believer, agnostic,
or frequent attender of the pew.

Everyone participates
and allowed whichever path to pursue.

All have the same rights,
the strong cannot the weaker subdue.

Rulers are elected not taking over by guns
through a coup.

Harmonious society is built,
the best picture humans drew.

The concept of democracy cannot be applied
in all facets of life.

People disagree, politicians argue much
like a husband and wife.

Genuine differences of opinions
is widespread and quite rife.

Some are simple; some are difficult
cause a struggle and strife.

These differences must be settled
through discussions not a knife.

Conductors decide who plays the flute
and who plays the fife.

Carpenters chisel chairs,
scientists study habitat and wildlife.

Businesses offer products, which to buy,
decided by housewife.

Need training, knowhow,
not everyone can operate a jackknife.

In any discipline there are many lay people
and few experts alive.

Not all what is popular is necessarily
absolutely correct and right.

What is true during the day could be
something different at night.

Just because we disagree,
does not mean we should have a fight.

Let us recognize subject matter experts
who are diligent and bright.

They are the people with the knowhow,
support them with all might.

Here majority cannot rule, experience
and knowledge has the oversight.

Pilots fly the planes; we can only
choose the destination and the flight.

Much made of our judicial system;
judges and lawyers who are upright.

Laws are better known by them,
not by the average people flying kite.

Lay people determining guilt or innocence,
should not see the light.

Hey, Dad: Are we Democrats or Republicans?

November 12, 2013

Hey Dad, are we Democrats or Republicans?

We are neither. We're independent Americans.

What is the difference? Can you tell me?

Well, it is not that easy Son, Trust me.

I hear Democrats are for big Government. Is that True?

What is big Government? It is hard to define or construe.

Aren't Republicans against taxes and regulations?

Well; that depends on the holders' imaginations.

Didn't Democrats support healthcare for all?

Yes, but that is an aim that is hard to install.

Do Republicans oppose abortion and the killing
of the unborn?
Not all of them. On this the entire population
is very much torn.

Do Republicans support the disadvantaged, the
poor, and the needy?
Some do. Most think, these people ask for
too much and greedy.

Do Democrats support more money for research
and education?
Yes, but that depends on the country's current
financial situation.

Republicans ask for tax reduction. Doesn't that shrink Government coffer?

Well yes, but that is the best a politician can do, when he has nothing else to offer.

But aren't Republicans for increase in military spending?

You see, local jobs in the politician's district need tending.

How come Democrats support increase in minimum wage, but shunned by Republicans?

Perhaps they fear the impact on labor cost and affect the demand for applicants.

Why Democrats support the big unions and cow tow to their demands?

They do that so that they will have more votes and to have the upper hand.

Do Democrats and Republicans agree on funding social security, Medicare and such?

Republicans want to reduce entitlements; Democrats say that can't be touched.

Our current economy is hurting and need lifting. Is there something to be done?

Democrats advocate more spending to stimulate the economy. Republicans agree to none.

Then what is the Republicans' solution for the current financial stagnation?

Control growth of the entitlements, remove regulations, and cut down on taxation.

Is there a hope that the two parties come together to find a common path for salvation?

These parties are too far apart on all the issues and agenda that concern the nation.

Dad, your answers are not clear and confusing. Are you running for a political position?

Maybe I should; I can't do more harm to the country and worsen its condition.

Your Vote Counts
VOTE

VOTE

Part D

The World

Honey, I killed an ant

May 27, 2008
New Jersey, USA

After having dinner, and spending some time watching the news, my wife heralded that it is time for our son to take a shower and go to bed. Part of my son's bedtime routine is that we read a book together. He reads a chapter and I read another one. We do this until we finish the book in a week or two. The current book we are reading is "The Red Badge of Courage" by Stephen Crane –a story about the American Civil War of the 1860s.

I went to the bathroom and while waiting for nature to take its course, I could hear the commotion my eight years old son was making in the shower on the floor above me. The exhaust fan was shielding some of the noise and gave me some relevant quietness that helped me enjoy my interlude with a natural chore which Mark Twain identified as one of the least appreciated pleasures.

While I was sitting on the seat and gazing on the wall and pondering the events of the day and regurgitating the recent news broadcast, something broke my deep concentration. A single tiny ant was making its way from underneath the basin toward the bathroom door. For a few moments, I mused at the way it was traveling –making left and right turns and zigzagging. But then a fear came over me. What if it managed to go outside and hide in the kitchen and finds food and invites many others? Oh no. This can't be. I quickly extended my left leg directly on top of it and applied overwhelming force to insure its demise. Yes, I killed it. I killed a tiny ant.

No sooner I did that, a strong feeling of remorse overcame me. How could I do this? I took a life. All what the ant wanted to do is to find food and to live. Why I could not let it share the crumbs that it could find? Oh Lord, please forgive me. Saddened and depressed I got out of the bathroom and headed upstairs where my wife saw me, and before she could comment on my condition, I confessed to her –"Honey, I killed and ant". I, who gave up eating meat for the last sixteen years so that I will not partake in slaughtering cows, sheep, and chickens, or killing fish; killed an ant. I found myself being a hypocrite for having my wife go through all the trouble of preparing separate version of the meal –one with and one without meat every day to accommodate my humanitarian posture. I remembered the sadness she and I feel when we see a dead deer alongside the road, or a flattened skunk or other animals overrun by cars. Then how could I explain what I did?

Looking into my wife's eyes, I could read what she was saying without uttering a word. I remembered days earlier, when she screamed out loud and summoned me to come to the kitchen. I hurried to her side and she pointed to the bottom of the open cupboard with hundreds of ants who had blackened a large area of the floor. She exclaimed these ants will ruin our house. Without hesitation, I reached for the Ant Killer spray can

on top of the refrigerator that we keep just in case along with other flying insect repellents and doused the entire bunch with a good coat of pesticide that rendered them all dead on the spot. With a paper towel, I cleaned the area and dumped the towel into the garbage can without giving it a second thought. I was satisfied that the problem was taken care of. Hamm; no guilty feeling there. What is the difference?

Searching for a rationale, I revisited the news I watched earlier in my mind. The news had two interesting segments. One about how a US Marine was caring for an orphan Iraqi child. To ensure his welfare, he enlisted the help of several of his comrades and sought assistance from the military establishment and other civilian agencies. He was able to arrange for the child to be treated in a hospital in the US since he could not be taken care of adequately in the war-torn Iraqi hospitals. The newscasters reacted approvingly and commented about how impressed they were by the marine's goodness and kind heartedness.

The earlier segment described how an air raid on a suspected Iraqi insurgents' hideout killed eighteen fighters and resulted in other casualties –the military calls them collateral damage. Among the dead were several civilians; some of which were children, old men, and women. No comments from the newscasters; but obvious approval of the outcome of the action taken by the American forces. Hiding among the civilian population and using simple weapons is considered a despicable act of cowardice. Throwing precision guided missiles from fighter jets miles above ground that kill indiscriminately is considered an act of courage.

In the book that my Son and I are reading there are tales of humanity and human feelings. What struck me about the Civil War was that it involved two armies of roughly equal strength and dedication to their cause who used similar tools and equipment. What gave one advantage over the other is better planning and strategic circumstances. I like to believe that the reason for the Union Armey prevailing is not because of their armaments; rather the strength of their argument.

Cranes book covers many human emotions and feelings. Group thinking and individual thought processes. The enemy far yonder whom one should hate and try to destroy and the foot soldier who is struggling to stay alive and hoping for the war to be over so that he could go back home to his family and loved ones. During the execution of the war, one comes across soldiers with similar hopes and aspirations. The wonder of humanity occasionally prevails when enemies extend helping hands to wounded or hungry soldiers from the other side.

When we look at people as a group, we think of them as things and not humans. It is them and us. But when we encounter individuals face to face, we see them as human beings. It is easier to see the commonality among us when we see the physical similarity between us and becomes easier to glance over the differences in what is inside our minds and hearts. I can see why the American administration prefers to harrow its enemy with 500-pound bombs from 5000 miles away rather than to sit at the table and negotiate with him face to face. ***Doing so, heavens forbid, could cause peace to break out.***

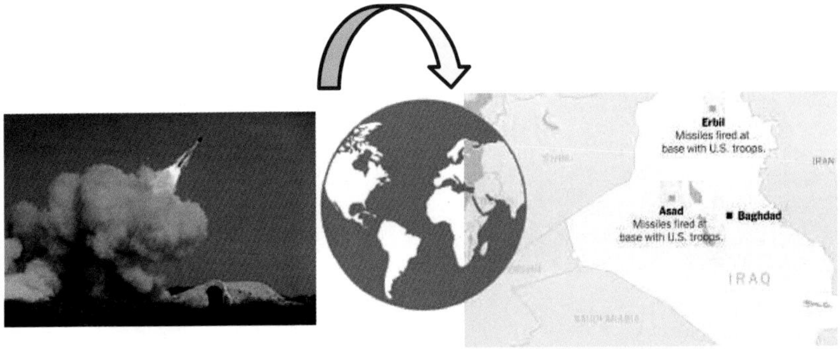
Erbil
Missiles fired at base with U.S. troops.
Asad
Missiles fired at base with U.S. troops.
Baghdad
IRAQ

History of the Arab-Israeli Conflict

September 4, 2013

Pictures were copied from www.google.com/images

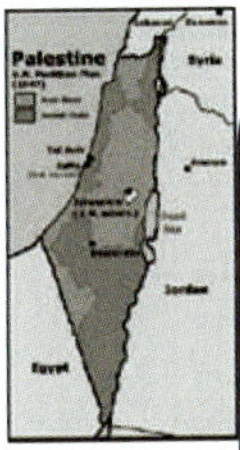

History of the Arab-Israeli Conflict

Much blood is being shed
in the Holy Land. Let me give
you some background.

I will tell you an incredible story.
It is not as strange and crazy
as it sounds.

After the Mongolian invasion,
the Arab glorious era rolled
down the mound.

Gone the days of scientific
advancements and philosophers
with great minds.

For over four centuries.
The Ottomans ruled, as Caliphs
they were crowned.

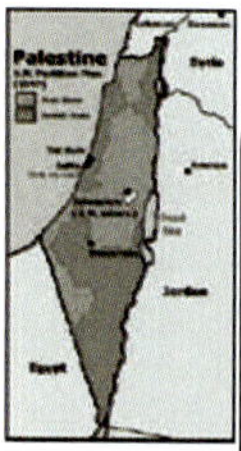

History of the Arab-Israeli Conflict

In World War One, the Ottomans were part of the Central Powers Alliance.

The Ottomans joined forces with Germany banking on its military appliance.

America joined forces with the British and the French, seeking compliance.

Italy was part of the Central Powers, but later dropped, for lack of reliance.

Germany had a strong military, good economy and enjoyed superior science.

History of the Arab-Israeli Conflict

During World War I, the British
sought the help of other forces
on the scene.

They solicited the oppressed people
to undermine their rulers
who were mean.

They lobbied the Arabs and
promised them self-rule that
they haven't seen.

They must rise against their piers.
In such an inner conflict
they haven't been.

The thirst for independence was
too great, from this situation
they must wean.

History of the Arab-Israeli Conflict

The British had a second front
to deal with in Europe
that needed attention.

How to undermine the economy
of the Germans and cause
internal tension.

They sought the help of the Zionists,
a historical fact, today
you can't mention.

Balfour promised Jews a homeland
in Palestine as if it
were his mansion.

Jews in Europe suffered under
the Christian rules found
hope for retention.

History of the Arab-Israeli Conflict

Arabs rose against the Ottomans
who subjugated them
for centuries prior.

They revolted against the Turks
in earnest, freedom and
liberty they desire.

War ended, the British reneged
on their promises that set
the Arabs on fire.

They had to control the situation,
they must appease and
the unrest was dire.

They divided the land in disparate
pieces and installed loyal
rulers for hire.

History of the Arab-Israeli Conflict

Arab territory that was liberated
from the Ottomans was
chopped in pieces.

French and British split the
spoils of the wars. The victor
can do as he pleases.

They created artificial countries
and gave themselves long
guardian leases.

Having divided countries weakens
the colonies and war threat
much decreases.

Oil was found in this land.
The value of this region
substantially increases.

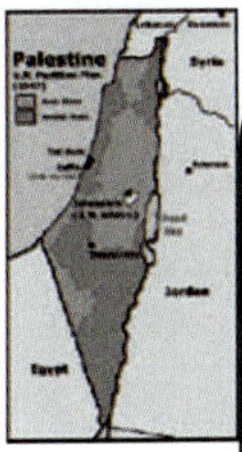

History of the Arab-Israeli Conflict

Zionists helped the Allies to defeat
the Germans sought to reap
their reward.

British couldn't outright do what
they promised; wanted
to break the accord.

Palestine was a land with
population. They were ruled
by religious sword.

How to let Jews move in without
displacing the natives
from their ward.

Yielding to the Zionists' demands
angers the Arabs, they
could not afford.

History of the Arab-Israeli Conflict

Zionists enticed the Jews to buy
Arab land in Palestine to
gain foothold out there.

They encourage Jews to move
to the Promised Land, there
was no time to spare.

By World War two, they managed
to amass six percent of the
total land's share.

Hitler's horrific atrocities against
the Jews was too much for
the World to bear.

Jewish settlement was accelerated,
try to stop it, or question it,
no one can dare.

History of the Arab-Israeli Conflict

Having the sympathy of the world,
they demanded a country
of their own.

England was between its
commitments to the Arabs
and the Zionists torn.

Secretly, they wanted to establish
a wedge in the Arab land,
a buffer zone.

They needed to control the oil fields,
ward off the Soviets,
the cornerstone.

A friction in the area will ensure
lasting prosperity for
the British throne.

History of the Arab-Israeli Conflict

Jews had bought six percent of
the land. They needed
this ratio to turn.

Militants terrorized the population;
they had to kill some
and others burn.

That caused the indigenous
inhabitants to be scared
and for fear to churn.

They abandoned their farms
and land, had no way their
livelihood to earn.

As refugees in neighboring lands,
return to their home they
desperately yearn.

History of the Arab-Israeli Conflict

Jewish terrorists began taunting
the British and haunting
the Palestinians.

They cared not what the world
would say, they controlled
their opinions.

After a while, the British
relinquished control and
gave up the dominions.

This made it easy for the gangs
to grab land from unarmed
poor civilians.

Now they had control of all
the valleys, climbing to the top
of the pavilions.

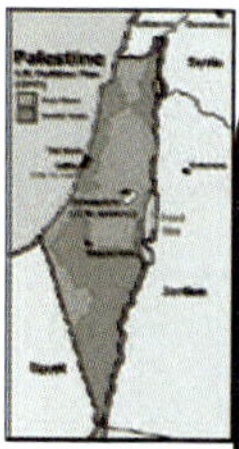

History of the Arab-Israeli Conflict

The terrorist gangs declared
Israel as a country and
sought recognition.

Arabs declared war against
the nascent nation hoping
for its demolition.

But the United Nation intervened
to stop the war, voted
for partition.

Arabs decline to recognize this
entity and vowed to cause
its abolition.

America rushed to grant
recognition and gave Jewish
settlers permission.

History of the Arab-Israeli Conflict

Ever since, Arab leaders promised
to help Palestinian refugees
to return Home.

We are Arabs, we are all brothers,
and we are one nation,
as the teeth of a comb.

These promises drove Arabs to
wars and in the process they
lost the holly Dome.

Arab people don't trust their
leaders. Their promises are
feckless as soap's foam.

Today Israel occupies all of the
Palestinian land and its tanks
there freely roam.

History of the Arab-Israeli Conflict

Arabs resorted to boycotts and
sanctions that were easily by
American thwarted.

Aid and arms is generously given
to Israel, its lobby is strong,
must be courted.

It is the sole democracy in the
Middle-East, it is our ally;
it must be supported.

Congress stands solidly behind
Israel, any decenter must be
exiled and deported.

No politician dares to speak ill of
Israel, this is the way it is,
must not be contorted.

History of the Arab-Israeli Conflict

Well, the Palestinian learned from
the Israelis founders, resorted
to armed terror.

They must fight for their rights.
This is the only way. Peace
preachers are in error.

Many innocent Israelis were killed.
This what you did to us look
in your mirror.

You took our land, you caused us
pain, we were displaced, gave
us much horror.

You have missiles, airplanes, tanks,
and guns, defeating you
requires a conjuror.

History of the Arab-Israeli Conflict

Then there was yet another war.
This time Israel suffered
some tactical defeat.

This paved the way for Egypt to
offer recognition, in exchange
to Israel's retreat.

Israel secured a peace treaty with
Egypt. Arab opposition was
strong and replete.

Palestinian resistance got stronger,
Israel realized, this headache
cannot be beat.

It was clear the Arab-Israeli peace
is far from being all inclusive
and complete.

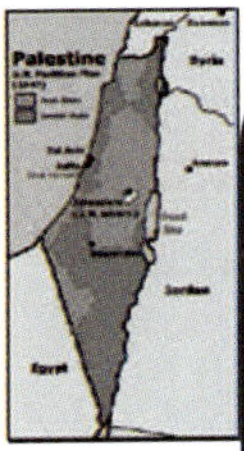

History of the Arab-Israeli Conflict

After years of bloody massacres,
sane people decided this war
should be over.

The horrific terror can no longer
be tolerated. Allow the peace
process to clover.

America sought peace between
the Israelis and the Arabs
needed a problem solver.

Secret talks were held. Some in
Europe. Some in Asia. And
some here in Dover.

This is not a small task. You cannot
use picks or shovels. You
need a land rover.

History of the Arab-Israeli Conflict

Peace deal between the Israelis and the Palestinians was drafted in Washington.

Palestinian resistance agreed to stop war and all terror activities fully abandon.

Israelis agreed to recognize Palestinians demand for self-rule just like Jordon.

However, they could not come to agreement on many issues. That's a big burden.

Occupation is continuing. The future of the peace is neither clear nor certain.

Conflict
Resolution

Robing Peter To Pay Paul

July 15, 2013

Image copied from www.google.com/images

Robbing Peter to Pay Paul

A modern phenomenon of robbing
Peter to Pay Paul.

A case in point that causes much
consternation and appall.

Palestinians paying for a horrific crime
which they had no role.

Their crime being an easy road on
which occupiers' tanks can roll.

Robbing Peter to Pay Paul

Please answer me; did the Arabs kill
six million Jews?

If not, then why are the Palestinians
paying these dues?

The holocaust was committed by
Germans? Read the news.

Thousands went to Palestine to eject
its occupants with no shoes.

Robbing Peter to Pay Paul

Well, why this particular land was chosen by the Zionist to conquer?

Jews need a homeland to own. An aim for generations they ponder.

They claim the return of Jews to the Promised Land they're really after.

These claims were made by secular nationalist not by religious master.

Robbing Peter to Pay Paul

Colonizers wanted the spoils of the war among themselves to divide.

They promised Palestine to the Zionist seeking victory and an easy ride.

They also promised the Arabs liberty if they rise, a promised that died.

After victory; the old empire was broken into puzzle pieces side by side.

Robbing Peter to Pay Paul

Came the Second World War; time to fulfill the promise not to be a liar.

They supported settlers in Palestine and allowed them weapon to acquire.

Organized Jewish militants terrorized the Arabs and set their homes on fire.

Thousands fled their homes and became refugees; their situation was dire.

Robbing Peter to Pay Paul

In the meantime, Zionist sympathizers in the West applied political pressure.

They had influence, they could vote, they had voice, they controlled treasure.

They could sway opinions; they can force Politicians to act at their pleasure.

Truman was persuaded to allow Jews to migrate to Palestine as a good measure.

Robbing Peter to Pay Paul

Two hundred thousand European Jews were allowed to migrate to Palestine.

Now, the land was thinned from native inhabitant, Zionist dream could shine.

Zionist declared Israel as the sovereign state. The West found it to be a good sign.

They needed a foothold to push the Soviets and force the Arabs to tow their line.

Robbing Peter to Pay Paul

Naturally, the rightful owners of the land
rose to fight the cruel intruder.

Arab countries joined the struggle; the
enemy was stronger and shrewder.

They were nascent countries with
limitations, Zionists were the better
shooter.

The U.N. intervened to stop the war.
Divided the land, gave half to the looter.

Robbing Peter to Pay Paul

The war ended in favor of the Zionists
entity, no surprise there to file.

Thousands were killed, other battered,
and millions sent away to exile.

The land was torn to pieces like a piece
of unwanted old piece of textile.

People's possessions were swallowed
and devoured by this hungry reptile.

Links to understand the issue of the Israeli-Palestinian conflict better.

http://en.wikipedia.org/wiki/History_of_Israel

http://history.state.gov/milestones/1945-1952/creation-israel

http://www.ifamericansknew.org/history/realstory.html

http://masbury.wordpress.com/2009/02/26/alfred-lilienthal-1949-israels-flag-is-not-mine/

http://en.wikipedia.org/wiki/Israel%E2%80%93United_States_relations

Time For TRANSPARENCY
TIME FOR JUSTICE
QUARTZ

The Second Holocaust

March 10, 2010

Jews - A People Victimized Twice

Images were copied from www.google.com/images

Jews - A People Victimized Twice

The Second Holocaust

Today's Germany; in an effort to cleanse itself from the stains of its horrific and barbaric treatment of its Jewish citizens and those of other European countries, during the Nazi era, goes out of its way to help and support Zionism and Israel; thinking that her blind support of the Jewish State will eradicate the past. This, of course is not so. The western world uses the Jewish people as a pawn in their dirty games to gain influence in the Middle East.

The Second Holocaust

These misguided and zealous Jews who primarily come from areas that were not affected by the Nazi atrocities, (The US, Russia, the Arab World, etc.) are committed and continue to commit similar acts of ethnic cleansing and subjugation against the Palestinians. In the process, today many Jews in Israel live in constant fear and are victims of terroristic acts by Palestinian extremists. They are living through a second holocaust. The western world managed to change the image of the Jews from victim to aggressor.

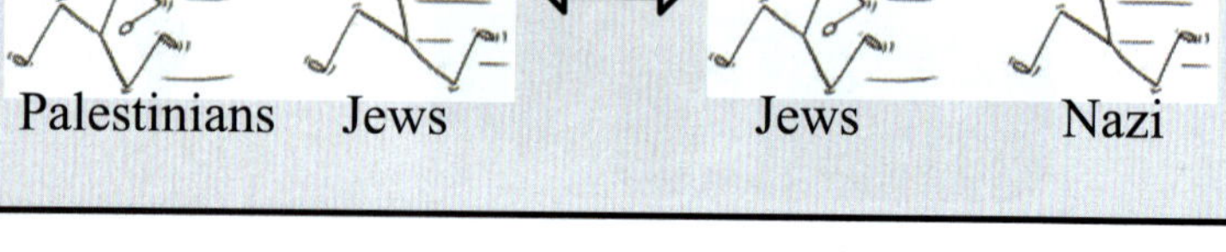

The Second Holocaust

Time, billions in financial aid to Israel, and its staunch support of Zionism have helped Germany and its people eradicate the gruesome and horrifying image that they have inherited from their Nazi past and gaining full acceptance in the modern civilization. I do not blame Germany for trying to erase this unflattering history. The German people have proven themselves to be above these events. But the way they try to cover over the past is harmful to a population that had nothing to do with the Holocaust -*See Robbing Peter to pay Paul*.

The Second Holocaust

It is time for not only Germany, but the entire world to come to the aid of both the Palestinian and the Jewish people and stop Israel's oppression of innocent Palestinian people in the name of Judaism.

The creation of Israel was supposed to offer the Jewish people a safe place to live. Did it? Israel since its creation in 1948, has gone through many wars. Thanks to the strong influence of the Jewish lobby in the United States and the United States strategic aims to keep the Arabs weak and divided so that they could control its natural resources -mainly oil; has, except for a few conflicts, won the war decidedly.

Jews - A People Victimized Twice

The Second Holocaust

During each conflict, Israel has increased the land that it occupies. With occupation, comes resistance and uprising. With each additional settlement, come international condemnation. Israel today is the most rebuked state in the United Nations. All UN Resolution against Israel are vetoed by the United States.

The Second Holocaust

The world has changed. Israel cannot rely on its Western patrons to survive. Eventually, the Palestinians and their supporters will gain parity, if not superiority with Israel, and come to the rescue of Justice. Although this view is farfetched today, seeing various Arab nations fallen under the spell of Israel and seeking normalization of relations. This might be happening on the leadership level, but the Arab population has not followed suit. In Egypt, after more than forty years of recognition of Israel, the Egyptian people still consider Israel as an enemy.

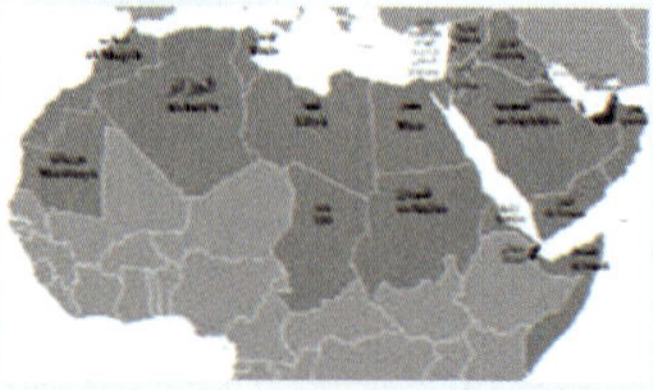

The Second Holocaust

Throughout the world Israel is considered as an oppressor regime. As a matter of fact, in many surveys, it was named the most hated nation in the world. Sadly, the US comes second. With the advent of the Internet, social media, and people having access to the current events and news, the atrocities committed by Israel are broadcast all over the world instantly.

Jews - A People Victimized Twice

The Second Holocaust

It has been more than seventy-five years since the end of World War II, not many survivors are alive today to remind people of the pain that that war inflicted on the innocent people who had committed no crime except for being Jews. Then when youngsters are reminded of these terrible events, they have a hard time reconciling what they hear with what they see Israel itself is doing to others innocent people who have no fault except being Arab.

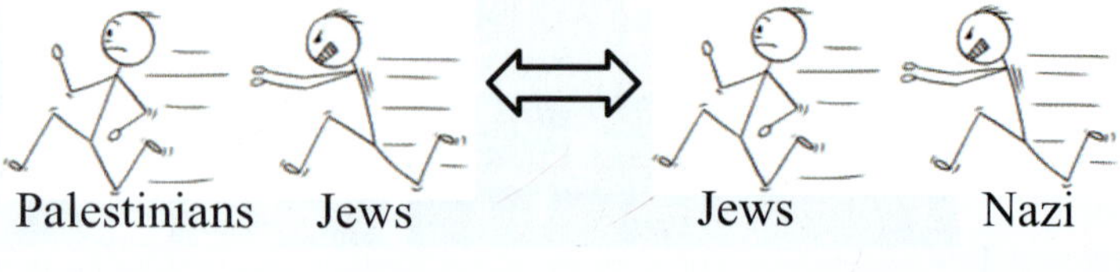

The Second Holocaust

So, what did the State of Israel offer the victims of the holocaust? More fear, more uncertainty, the animosity of a larger population in the world. Israel's population is a little over 9 million today (March 2020). Of this 74.2% are Jews, and 20.9% are Arabs. The Arab world has a population of around 422 million. The muslim population, including the Arabs, is 1.9 billion. Add to that the third world nations who mostly sympathize with the Palestinian cause. If ever, the US abandon Israel, Israel is left to face this enormous hostile population.

The Second Holocaust

With the dissolution of the Soviet Union, the decrease of demand for oil, one might wonder if America will ever abandon Israel. Well Israel served its purpose in the past. The US must compete with other rising powers in the world such as China, India, Japan, South Korea, the European Union, and Russia for access to resources, other than oil, and to gain market share for its products & services. It stands to reason, that it would modify its absolute blind support of Israel and move toward a more evenhanded policy in the Arab-Israeli conflict.

Jews - A People Victimized Twice

The Second Holocaust

Iran, Iraq, Syria, Algiers, Tunisia, and possibly other government in the Arabian Peninsula (which are facing financial crises), would join effort to neutralize Zionism and free the Palestinian people from the shackles of oppression and the scourge of occupation.

Jews today, weather living in Israel or outside, are suffering from two holocausts. One at the hand of the Nazis and Two: currently being labeled oppressor or supporter of oppression of the Palestinian people. The image of being a victim is replaced with oppression of others, ethnic cleansing, subjugation, and cruelty.

The Second Holocaust

Jews - A People Victimized Twice

From time to time, a conflict flares up. Israel's enemies begin lobbing missiles across its borders. To protect the population, the Government of Israel directs its people to hide in underground shelters. This is repeated many times over the last few years. Is this a life the Jewish people were looking for when they moved to Palestine? Of course, Israel retaliates with heavy bombing of Palestinian resistance and cause yet another horrifying result that kills innocent women and children and give Israel another bad image.

The Second Holocaust

To put a stop to this vicious cycle of violence, Israel must come to terms with the realities of the world and try to find a solution to live in peace with its cousins - (Arabs and Jews are both descendants of the Prophet Ibrahim). The last chapter of this book, "***Salt & Pepper -a Recipe for Peace***", offer a possible solution.

Syria

September 4, 2013

Syria

There is much fuss and uproar about the regime in the Arab country of Syria.
The clamor and call for war is defining and the rage approaching hysteria.
Hundreds of thousand people died in the last two years, count them Victoria.
These are innocent men, women, and children not some kind of bacteria.
Ask why this all happened? There is no explanation. Much like Assyria*[1].

[1]Assyria: One of the old names of the current country called Iraq.

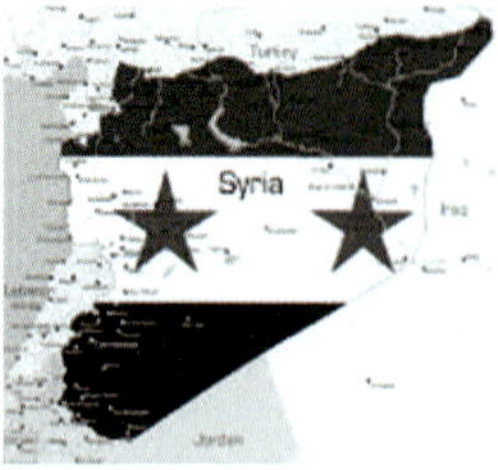

Syria

The drums of war are not to entertain,
but to satisfy the thirst of vampires.
They must have blood. They do not care
how much devastation they sire.
Outsiders use their money to influence
the media and mercenaries to hire.
They speak of freedom; but really the
destruction of the country they desire.
To cause turmoil and chaos in the country,
sectarian fighting they inspire.

Syria

Who is this vampire we speak of? Is he real
or a fiction of our imagination?
Is he a person, a secret group of people,
or a devil within a foreign nation?
The answer is obvious and clear. Who is
the beneficiary of this formation?
Arabs who lived for many years under
cruel rulers and suffered stagnations.
Overnight they turned into revolutionaries.
Spring? After years of dehydration!

Syria

There is a grander plan is unfolding in this
very important part of the world.
Who is benefiting from the chaos? Surely,
not the people, but, the war lord.
Divided and weakened Arab countries,
to their foe a greater security afford.
Arabs engaged in self-destruction, is sweeter
than inoperable peace accord.
This must be said: what unites the Arab
people is their culture not the sword.

Syria

Soon, the Arabs will awaken from their
hibernation and gain their sanity.
They cannot remain to be entranced in their
glorious past that is an oddity.
They must recognize the changing world
and thrust forward to join society.
To gain strength, they must respect their
tradition, but give others parity.
Reciting the fable of single stick and a
bundled branch, applying it is a rarity*2.

**2There was an old man on his deathbed who had eight sons. The sons were always feuding. The man wanted to teach his sons a listen. He gave then a bunch of 8 sticks that were tied together and asked each son to try to break them. None could. So, he untied the stick and gave each one a single stick and asked them to break the stick now. They all could. So, he turned to them and said: "I hope you learned a listen. If you are united nobody can defeat you. But if you are each on your own, you can easily be broken."*

Syria

Arab nations must set aside their differences
and march toward unity.
They have much to gain working in harmony
to build their community.
Strength they'll gain when they are united,
that'll give them immunity.
Peace and stability will bring about progress,
prosperity, and impunity.
All must help this dream to come true and
give peace an opportunity.

Articles

Salt and Pepper

A RECIPE FOR PEACE

Musa Marashi - Author of Sharing Thoughts

Below is the Preface for a book I have been working on since 1995. It was updated in 2019.

Nuevo Geo
(The New World)
Preface

As we embrace a new millennium and nineteen years into the new century, the world is facing escalation of old conflicts, emergence of new troubles, and many of the issues of the past century remain unresolved. The main reason for that is that we (the people of the Earth) have not had the courage to overcome many of the hang-ups that remained with us from the inception of our so-called civilization until now. These hang-ups are, if looked at objectively (I acknowledge that objectivity is a subjective matter) you see that they are routed in belief systems that are man-made and are quite artificial. Concepts such democracy, patriotism, nationalism, religion, social order, justice, rule of law, country, family, home, sportsmanship, free market, commerce, globalization, international relationship, security, peace, and so on and so on; are open to scrutiny and revision.

What Nuevo Geo addresses is a new approach in resolving many of the existing world difficult and intransigent conflicts. It also touches upon how to better manage some of the social issues facing our societies. These solutions are based on practicality and are inspired by what is going on and what is being practiced in other segments of our society that could be used as a model for solving similar, but unrelated, problems.

What drives me to write this book is: conflicts such as the Middle East (the Palestinian-Israeli issue), the Kurds in Turkey, Kashmir, Northern Ireland, Cyprus, and host of other conflicts in the world. I believe, I owe it to my fellow human beings to write this book, Perhaps, this out-of-the-box thinking could be adopted to relieve humanity from sufferings, injustices, and the bane of wars.

Musa Marashi

Fictitious TV Interview

My dream is to see the world in peace and harmony. People of different creed, race, national origin, and gender live together and deal with each other in fairness and balance. In the past, I thought of having a TV interview with maybe David Frost, Larry King, Charlie Rose, or Fareed Zakaria to share my proposal. Unfortunately, I was not able to receive permission to include them in my fictitious interview. I am approaching 75 years of age and I want to spread the word. I opted to use a media icon to accomplish my mission. My hope is this fictitious interview with Edward R. Marrow (who has long been deceased) helps me explain the ***Salt and Pepper*** proposal.

This is a fictitious interview

My next guest has proposed a new approach for solving international conflicts. He explains his approach in his book titled "Nuevo Geo". I welcome the author Musa Marashi.

Welcome to the show.

Thank you . Glad to be here.

This is a fictitious interview

What kind of problems are you trying to solve?

Hopefully, the most intransigent ones. Such as the Arab-Israeli conflict, The Kurdish aspiration for independence, the Indian-Pakistani issue concerning Kashmir, Cyprus, etc.

How do you propose to do that?

Let me explain the proposal by tackling one conflict at a time.

This is a fictitious interview

Fine.

Let me talk about the Arab-Israeli conflict first, since that is the one, I am most familiar with.

Go ahead.

Regardless of the historical claims and facts that divide these two parties, there were many attempts made to reconcile the differences between the parties which all failed.

You refer to the most recent effort between the Late Palestinian leader Arafat and former Israeli Prime Minster Ehud Barak which was mediated by President Clinton!

That and many other subsequent efforts.

This is a fictitious interview

Why do you think these efforts failed?

They did not address the main issues that both parties were concerned about.

Could these issues be resolved through direct negotiation?

I don't think so. The issues that separate the two parties could not be solved using the current framework.

You mean the Two-State solution?

Yes.

This is a fictitious interview

But that the stated position of the United States and its allies, the U.N., and the two parties.

I understand. Look how far it has gone without a meaningful resolution.

What do you think it should be done?

Well, let us identify the most difficult issues that the parties could not agree on.

- **First: Borders**
- **Second: The Status of Jerusalem**
- **Third: Right of Return for the Palestinian Refugees.**
- **Fourth: Settlements**

But Israel wants security. You did not name that as one of the issues.

I agree. However, you are concerned with security when you live among enemies. Perhaps you may not need it when you are living among friends and allies.

This is a fictitious interview

Are you proposing to make the Arabs and the Israelis allies?

In time they could. They need to work hard at it.

I like to see that. OK, how do we get there?

First, we need to dispose of several concepts that causing much human suffering such as: Countries with Borders, National Identity versus State Association, etc.

What do you mean?

Let us take for instance you and I are citizens of the United States. We carry its Passport to travel, and we recognize its borders to be the fifty states and the territories.

This is a fictitious interview

Go on.

Here in the United States we believe that we all, except the Native Americans, came from somewhere else. So we are familiar with the terms Irish-American, Italian-American, African-American, etc.

But we swear allegiance to this country, right?

Indeed. My point is, that all of us believe that we have the right to all what this country has to offer and that we are equal. So, the Native Americans and you and I have the same rights.

But we recognize the limited sovereignty of the Native Americans in their own reservation.

Yes. Thank you. That is another point I would like to use to support my proposal. However, I would like to point out the relationship between the American Catholic and the Vatican.

This is a fictitious interview

You mean the Pope?

Yes, yes. This especially becomes evident, when a new Pope is being chosen. It seems all Catholics, and for that matter, the rest of us, will focus on who will become the new Pope. During that time, we all become Catholics.

You're right.

My point is, as a practicing Catholic, one could have allegiance to the Church and its leader outside of the borders of the Vatican.

OK. What does that mean?

This means, that borders can not define people. Their belief, their language, their culture, and their shared experiences that defines them.

This is a fictitious interview

Are you proposing to get rid of all borders?

That would be great. But no. I am suggesting to separate national identity from border identity.

How?

Here in America, we recognize dual citizenship for some countries, if not all. I believe this has to do with reciprocity. Anyway, most first, and some second-generation Americans, still identify themselves with their country of origin. They speak its language, they practice their way of life, they consume the food from their native countries, etc. That is why, we have such a rich choice of ethnic and exotic foods from all over.

This is a fictitious interview

We don't force them to eat our food (whatever that is), or follow our religion, adopt our culture, etc. We simply ask any newcomer to adhere to our civil laws and regulations and respect our constitution. The constitution gives all equal right and equal protections. It separates the State from the Church. It gives us freedom to speak, freedom to worship, and pursue whatever that makes us happy that is lawful. Being American does not prevent us from identifying ourselves as Irish, Italian, Polish, Arab, or Jewish.

We give the right to people to be who they want to be.

That is right. People yearn for identity. I believe, that is what makes us pursue careers, follow educational paths, enjoy certain music, identify with sports teams, etc. There is an innate desire for us versus them. In this country we have almost limited it to political affinity and economic status. We still do have racial problems, but I am hoping we will get rid of it in time.

This is a fictitious interview

How does the desire for identity relate to the Arab-Israeli conflict?

That is the main driver of this conflict. Israel has managed to attract many Jews from all over the world to live in Palestine. Some were attracted for the Jewish identity of the State – these are mainly secular Jews. Some other Jews (Orthodox) who may not recognize Israel as a state (The Promised Land), but associate Israel with its religious relevance to their faith.

How about the Palestinians?

The Palestinians are also seeking their own identity. Over 20% of the Israeli population is Arab. And of course, there are more than five million living in the West Bank and Gaza. More than two million Palestinians live in refugee camps throughout the Arab world.

This is a fictitious interview

That is the reason for the Two-States solutions, right?

Well that does not solve the problem. Back to the list of issues that prevented any lasting settlements for the conflict.

So, what do you propose?

I propose the creation of a single entity which has the borders of the recognized territory of Palestine prior to the creation of Israel. Then allow two elected governments to operate from this territory. One for the Israelis and the other for the Palestinians.

Do you mean two countries with the same border?

Yes. But these countries represent the National Identity of the people living within that border.

This is a fictitious interview

How would that work? Who will be responsible for the normal functions of the government such as security, law and order, education, infrastructure, etc.?

There will be a single government that is responsible for the administrative part of the government. This government will be elected by the total population and approved by the two national governments.

What would the two national governments do?

They issue national identity, passports, enact civil laws for their respective populations.

So, there would be one Government called Israel and the other called Palestine living inside a single border?

Yes. So a Jewish person living in the same territory can carry an Israeli identification, travel using an Israeli passport, and follow the laws that are compatible with Judaism.

This is a fictitious interview

Similarly, an Arab person can carry a Palestinian identification and travel using a Palestinian passport. Since there are Christian Arabs and Muslim Arabs, then each could follow the laws that pertain to him or her.

You are telling me that there are three different governments ruling the same territory? Wouldn't this be confusing?

Both communities require garbage collection, paved roads, protecting the environment, managing the food supply, etc. All these functions are common to both communities. You are not going to design a road differently, whether you are an Arab or a Jew.

So, what is the purpose of the National Government?

This allows all citizens of the land to live anywhere they want, while preserving their identity. This solves two major issues, which are the borders and the settlements. There would be no border dispute and the settlements could remain where they are; since they are not violating any borders. This also gives the Arabs who live in the current Israeli proper the chance to join their brethren who live in the West Bank and Gaza.

This is a fictitious interview

Now I can see this solution will also satisfy all the national extremist on both sides. Those who believe that the entire land of Palestine belongs to the historic Judea and Samaria and the Hamas faction who refuses to forfeit any part of original Palestine.

Indeed.

But this could never be done. It is not the normal way of running governments. How can you ensure harmony among these people?

Please remember this. Eastern Jews lived among Arabs and Muslim in peace for many centuries. They played an important part in shaping the culture, advancing the scientific developments, conducting trade, and every other aspect of these societies. There is no reason to think they cannot go back to that way of living side by side. I can give you many anecdotal evidence of how Jews from Iraq, Syria, Egypt, Morocco, and other Arab countries speak fondly of their memories of living in these countries.

This is a fictitious interview

OK, you addressed the border and the settlements issues. How about the other two that you mentioned?

Let us talk about Jerusalem. Since the country is identified as both Arab and Israeli, then there is no reason to think of dividing the city. The Israeli government could have its capital there and the Palestinians could have their capital there as well.

You think this could be acceptable to both sides?

Well, I hope so. The fourth issue is the status of the refugees. Since the return of the refugees does not have impact on status of the Israeli (Jewish) population, they could return to their homeland. Not many of them will return. Many Arab countries withheld recognition of children born in the refugee camps as citizens, now they can do so, because the issue is no longer needed to pressure Israel.

This is a fictitious interview

Are you proposing they return to their homes prior to the 1948 War?

No, not necessarily to their original homes, which may not exist anymore, but to somewhere in the Palestinian proper. For those who lost their farms, homes, business, etc., a compensation plan can be devised so that they can live elsewhere in the country.

How about security?

Well, Israel has amassed a huge military arsenal over the years. The Palestinian could benefit from this military advantage to assert themselves as a regional power among the Arab countries. In the first decade or so, security of this country should be delegated to the Israelis. After a passage of time, when the Jewish population is at ease with its Arab cohabitants, the Arab population can gradually share that responsibility.

This is a fictitious interview

Ok, you addressed the four issues. But I still can't see how this really works.

Do you remember from your high school chemistry. Where we learned about substances could be solutions or mixtures. Solutions are made from two or more elements interacting with each other to produce that substance. Elements are dissolved (interact) to produce the solution. The solution has a completely different characteristics than its constituent elements. For example combing Hydrogen with Chloride produces Hydrochloric Acid (HCl), which is not like either the Hydrogen or the Chloride.

On the other hand, air is a mixture of several gases. To better understand this idea, let us think of mixing salt and paper place them in a jar, they will occupy the same space but each of them preserve its identity and characteristics.

So, you are suggesting a Salt and Pepper solution?

Yes.

This is a fictitious interview

I can see evidence of different people living in the same area, here in the United States. You have Queens, New York. It has many sections which are predominantly populated by certain ethnic groups. You have Koreans, Indians, Chinese, Spanish, neighborhoods. And, all live-in harmony.

Yes, that is right.

But this does not mean that each group has its own government. They all are subject to the laws of the government of the United States.

True, but there are three other governments that the citizens of Queens can elect and are subject to its rules – the State, the City, and the Borough.

This is a fictitious interview

You are right. But, each level of government has its own laws and they take precedence over other laws. For example federal laws override state laws. State laws override city laws, etc. Some laws are exclusively within the domain of the states and federal enforcement has no jurisdiction over these laws.

You are right. So, there is a vertical arrangement of the structure of the government. I am proposing a horizontal one. The horizontal arrangement will preserve the character of the population being governed.

OK, supposed the Palestinians and the Israelis agreed to this formula, what about the rest of the Arab and Muslim world?

If all the Palestinian factions agree to this, there would be no reason for the Arabs to continue their hostile stand toward Israel. The old enemy, Israel, is now the new member-Palestine.

This is a fictitious interview

One only could hope. How about the Jewish population of Israel, wouldn't they be fearful of Arabs moving to their neighborhood, now that anyone can live anywhere, he or she want?

They shouldn't. Think about it. As Americans we can live anywhere, we want. But you don't see people from the Bronx moving to Beverly Hills.

Is there a peace dividend that both the Israelis and the Palestinians can gain from this?

That is for sure. Palestinians and Arabs in general can benefit from the technical and scientific advances that the Israelis have made. The Israelis can benefit from the extended market that the Arab world can offer. The combination of science, natural resources, investments, and geographic position of this unity will be a formidable economic force to recon with.

This is a fictitious interview

Do you think this is an easier way to solve the Arab-Israeli conflict than the normal channels of negotiation?

Normal channels of negotiation cannot produce a lasting and durable peace that is fair to all sides. So long one side is dependent on the total support of the biggest power in the world, it will not find it necessary to compromise. Similarly, the weaker party cannot forfeit its legitimate rights and the rights of those who have been displaced without losing its legitimacy.

But we have a case of Northern Ireland. Negotiation did produce a peace accord.

With all due respect to the effort made by the US and the UK, the Northern Ireland issue was not resolved until both parties realized that they both will become part of the European Union. So, their need for identity will become moot. I believe, the creation of the European Union had a lot to do to move the peace process in Northern Ireland forward.

This is a fictitious interview

What evidence do you have that this solution would be acceptable to both the Arabs and the Israelis?

It is the twenty first century. We must look for solutions that are new. Living in constant state of war and fear of annihilation is not a normal condition that a nation should live under. Occupation is not a solution for this problem. The issues I listed earlier, could only be resolved under this scheme.

Didn't Muammar Gaddafi propose such a solution as well?

No, his solution was a single government for a state which its name will be a combination of the two names. What I am proposing is to preserve each nationality to live not alongside each other as separate entity, but rather as a two people sharing the same land with the right to live anywhere, they want, while having their own laws and national identity.

This is a fictitious interview

Do we have an example anywhere in the world either today or in the past that such a solution has been attempted?

I venture to say the United States is an example of that. Not by allowing each nationality to issue its own passports and enact its own laws, but in everything else. For example, in many countries the government provides many of the services. Where in the United States we have multiple private companies competing to do that –examples are insurance, express mail, healthcare, etc.

As far as the form of government, we have federal system with several states that run their own governments. In the UK, they have monarchy. Both systems work. The common thread is that both are democracies. This solution will work for the Arab-Israelis only if they were democracies. Now, they seem to be so.

So, democracy is a pre-requisite for this?

Yes

This is a fictitious interview

I'm still wondering if such an arrangement even works?

Well, let us look at the motor vehicle registrations laws in say New Jersey versus California. In California, the plate goes with the purchase of the car, whereas in New Jersey, the driver owns the plate. In California, most of the roads are toll free, whereas in New Jersey you must pay a toll for its major highways. The systems are different, but they both work.

In the Catholic Church, there is a single hierarchy ending with the Pope. In Shia Islam, you supposed to follow a religious leader, the equivalent of a pope. You can choose among a number of these leaders who publish their interpretation of the Islamic law and upon evaluation, you decide whom to follow.

These are the Ayatollahs?

Yes

This is a fictitious interview

Interesting.

In many countries they drive on the left side of the road, while other drive on the right side of the road.
In some cultures, the woman gives dowry to the man to marry. In other cultures, it is the man who gives dowry to the woman. In most western countries, neither of these traditions are in effect. In Malaysia they have several kings, the king is elected and rules on a rotational basis. Most monarchs inherit their positions. In the western world, the monarch is a titular leader. In most of the rest of the world, the King has absolute power.

What I am driving at, is that there are many ways to runs things. We must invent new ways to solve our most stubborn issues.

And you think this approach will do that?

Yes

This is a fictitious interview

What benefit would the peace between the Israelis and the Palestinians will produce for the Arab world?

Many Arab leaders have used the Palestinian issue as diversion to hide their shortcomings. They use this issue to cover up their failures or to justify their harsh rules. They hide behind the Palestinian issue to suppress any opposition or challenges to their dictatorial regimes by claiming national security concerns and the larger Arab cause.

But some Arab countries recognized Israel. Others are still rejecting peace.

Yes, there are two Arab camps. Those who reject peace with Israel so long it is occupying Arab lands and has settlements in the West Bank. Off course, the Arabs will have a hard time accepting Jerusalem in the hand of the Israelis. They also demand the return of the Refugees to their former homes.

This is a fictitious interview

These are the four issues you talked about earlier. Then what do the Arabs disagree about?

The two camps basically agree on these issues. However, they disagree on the method of attaining these goals. The first camp is the resistance camp, this includes, Syria, Lebanon, Algiers, and Tunisia. Iraq used to be part of this camp. However, at this moment, it is militarily too weak to have an influence. Off course, with the downfall of Kaddafi, Libya's stance is not clear.

The other camp is the moderate camp which is led by Saudi Arabia, the Gulf countries, Jordon, Morocco, and others. Egypt, which spearheaded the peace process with Israel, is undergoing a reevaluation of its peace agreement with Israel. The people of Egypt were always suspicious of this treaty and along with the rest of the Arab populations in other Arab countries totally reject the State of Israel. The evidence of this is quite clear. The Egyptian government signed a peace treaty with Israel more than twenty-five years ago; but the Egyptian people still consider Israel as an enemy.

This is a fictitious interview

Why can't the Arabs accept Israel? It is a legitimate state that recognized by the UN, and most countries of the world.

Let me give you a parallel example. Today we have more than 12 million undocumented people living in the United States. These primarily came through the Mexican border seeking a better life for themselves and their families. Many have had children here. They contribute to the economy of this nation. However, most American politicians, I assume reflecting the sentiments of their constituents, do not want to offer a path to citizenship to them. Now, let us remember this, we all are immigrants or sons of immigrants. We all came from somewhere else. But, we (I mean those who object to giving the undocumented aliens a path to citizenship) are not willing to grant the same opportunity to these undocumented immigrants.

Not many Americans know the facts about the creation of the State of Israel. The Arab population knows these facts well. These facts are taught in the schools, passed on from parent to children, mentioned in the media, part of their cry for equality and justice. They cannot readily accept a population that mainly came from Europe and America to settle in Palestine.

This is a fictitious interview

Return to their promised land.

Ok, suppose if an American family found out that the home they own was built on top of a burial ground of some Native American tribe. And, that tribe is laying a claim on that house, would the family relinquish its home?

Maybe not. But Israel now is over seventy years old. It has over five million population. You clearly don't suggest that these people should leave?

No. I believe all people have the right to live anywhere in the world that they like. But that should not be at the expense of others. In the case of Israel, there were thousands of Palestinians who were killed and millions more who were forced to flee to live as refugees in other parts of the Arab world to make room for refugees from Europe and immigrant from the rest of the world.

This is a fictitious interview

But the Jews were also persecuted. There were more than six millions who died in the Holocaust.

True. But, can I ask you, did the Palestinians commit these atrocities or the Germans?

No, of course the Germans.

Then why do the Palestinians have to pay the price?

I guess both people suffered a tragedy in their own way.

Yes, but the victims of the Holocaust received a better treatment than the Palestinians.

This is a fictitious interview

What can America do more to help solve this problem? It is trying to reach a peace settlement between the Israelis and the Palestinians.

That effort is doomed to failure. Because it is based on unjust and unrealistic expectations from the Palestinians and the Arabs at large.

So what do you suggest the American Government should do?

First thing is to show equal concerns to the Palestinian issues as it does to the Israeli lobby.

But Israel is our most stanch ally in the region. It is democratic and we share most common things.

This is the rhetoric that the pro-Israeli lobby dispenses.

This is a fictitious interview

You don't think it is true?

Not for a moment. American support for Israel puts America at odds with not only the Arabs, but with the Muslim world and the third world at large. What you hear from the mouths of the officials is not the reflection of the sentiment of the population.

How so?

Well, if you review all the surveys done in the world, you will find that Israel is ranked as the most hated country in the world and America comes second.

How can we change that?

My proposal may help to do that.

This is a fictitious interview

You seem to believe this could be done. Ok, assuming that was done, then what next?

You asked me earlier what would be the impact on the Arab world, if the Israelis and the Palestinians decide to live together under the Salt & Pepper plan, I believe that would have a substantial impact on the region. The threat of a conflict with Israel is gone, the Arabs will focus their effort on unity. To achieve that, they need to follow the model of the Israelis and the Palestinians.

You are thinking of uniting the Arab countries?

Yes.

Would Israel be part of this mix?

Yes. Both Israel and the Arabs will benefit from this arrangement. A united Arab entity with all its resources fortified by the advancements of the Israelis will be a formidable power.

This is a fictitious interview

Wouldn't this entity compete with the US?

No, it would be a stronger economical and strategic partner to balance the Chinese and other Asian and European powers.

Why couldn't the Arabs unite in all these years?

During the cold war, many Arab countries were dominated by regimes that were supported either by the Soviet Union or the West. They were pawn in the game of influence.

How can you convince the American to follow this plan?

First, we need to assuage the Israeli lobby. Second, we need to alert the American government of the Arab and Muslim resentment for neglecting the plight of the Palestinians, which has caused many of the headaches that America and its allies are facing today.

This is a fictitious interview

You mean terrorism?

Indeed. You see, Arabs believe that America is like a father who divorced his wife and married a young woman and asking his children to love her, even though she is cruel and hurtful toward them. His wife could do no wrong, while the children are punished for raising objection to this vicious and deceitful woman. Once, America recognizes that and finds an avenue to please both the Israeli lobbies and the Arabs, then we shall have peace here at home and in the Middle-east. Sorry, but this is the reality. In my forty-nine years in this country, never once I heard Israel being condemned or questioned about any of its maltreatments against the Palestinians. It is obvious, the politicians and the media are controlled by the Israeli lobby. However, I am greatly impressed with the courage of so many fair-minded Jews, who are themselves children of the Holocaust, who speak out against Israeli policies. That why, I am hopeful that eventually a sense of fairness will prevail, and we will move toward peace.

As a matter of fact, I believe that Jews are being subjected to a second Holocaust. And that is the way this population is being viewed as either the oppressor or supporter of the oppressor (Israel). Israeli actions toward the Palestinians is overshadowing the memory of the Holocaust.

This is a fictitious interview

But support for Israel is natural. They want to provide security for the Jewish people in their own country that they have a historical link to. They want to prevent another Holocaust. How could they forget about the land they were driven from? Many Jews yearn to return to the land of Israel.

Most Jews live in Western countries in security and peace. It is the Jewish population that lives in Israel which is under constant threat of war. So, Israel did not bring peace to the Jews. It brought them five wars in the span of seventy years.

About the Jews yearning to return to the land of Israel. Remember this is a historical fact that is more than three thousands years old. How come you want to support that but not the yearning of the Palestinian refugees who were driven only seventy or so years ago from their homeland?

This is a fictitious interview

So, should Jews abandon their hope to one day live in their promised land?

Not at all. Under my proposal, they are free to do so. They would have access to all the land of Judea and Samaria, and not limited to the current Israeli proper.

So your solution will benefit all and bring peace to the world.

At least to the Middle-East and other parts of the world.

Do you think this model will work for other conflicts as well?

Yes

This is a fictitious interview

Let us talk about Kashmir.

My proposal for Kashmir is to recognize Kashmir as an independent administrative entity that simultaneously belongs to both India and Pakistan. This entity could enact its own laws to manage its affairs. Its inhabitants can choose to identify themselves as Pakistanis of Indians and hold their Passports. They can follow the laws of their respective countries for personal and religious affairs.

Ok, how about the Kurds?

You know the Kurds were distributed among four countries –Turkey, Iraq, Iran, and Syria. They have no country of their own. Except, after the downfall of the Saddam regime, the new Iraqi constitution allowed the predominately Kurdish provinces in northern Iraq to federate and form their own independent region.